rororo

ro
ro
ro

rororo Sprachen

Herausgegeben von Ludwig Moos

Fast jeder, der Englisch als zweite Sprache spricht, macht Fehler, die für seine muttersprachliche Herkunft typisch sind. Hatte *Better Your English* (rororo sprachen 60802) zum Ziel, die gängigsten Fehler zu verlernen, so hilft *Perfect Your English* die versteckten Fallen zu umgehen, in die wir Deutschen gerne tappen. Mit einer unterhaltsamen Story und pfiffigen Übungen entwickeln Sie das Sprachgefühl, mit dem Sie sich ungefährdet im Englischen bewegen.

Dr. René Bosewitz ist native speaker und leitet eine Sprachschule in Heidelberg. Zusammen mit Robert Kleinschroth hat er bei rororo sprachen *Joke Your Way Through English Grammar* (8527) und *Joke by Joke to Conversation* (8795) veröffentlicht, außerdem in der Reihe Business English *Manage in English* (60137), *Better than the Boss* (60138), *How to Phone Effectively* (60139), *Drop Them a Line* (60261, mit Bryan Hemming), *Test Your Management Skills* (60260), *Get Through at Meetings* (60262), *Let's Go International* (60267), *Check Your Language Level* (60268), *Business English from A to Z* (60269, mit Bryan Hemming), *The Way Things Work* (60369), *How to Read the Business Press* (60506), *Small Talk for Big Business* (60439) und *Business by Jokes* (60721), *Sell like Hell* (60722), *Master Your Business Phrases* (60725), *Get to Grips with Company English* (60845), *Spice up Your Speeches* (60804), *Master Your Business Phrases* (60725) und *Better Your Business English* (60846).

René Bosewitz

Perfect Your English

Wie man die tückischsten Sprachfallen vermeidet

Illustrationen Mathias Hütter

Rowohlt Taschenbuch Verlag

A special thanks to Annette for her help and support in this project. Without her it would not have been possible.

Originalausgabe
Veröffentlicht im Rowohlt Taschenbuch Verlag GmbH,
Reinbek bei Hamburg, Februar 2001

Umschlaggestaltung Büro Hamburg, Susanne Reizlein
(Illustration Gerd Huss)
Layout Anne Drude
Satz Stone PostScript, QuarkXPress 3.31
Druck und Bindung Clausen & Bosse, Leck
Printed in Germany
ISBN 3 499 61147 3

The Contents

Foreword

Perfect Your English is the follow-up book to *Better Your English*. It has the same intention as *Better Your English* – to identify and eliminate typical German mistakes in English.

If you read *Better Your English* you'll already know our hero, Ernst Lachnit. A year ago Ernst made the effort to "better" his English. He attended the Volkshochschule and then went off to "little" England on an intensive language course in Canterbury which is pretty near the continent. We observed Ernst during this period of enlightenment and we laughed along with him as he made those mistakes which are so typical of all of us. During that time, too, "Laughnot" developed a little love for the island and a greater love for one of the "island monkeys", or rather for a lady monkey, Jenny.

Once again we meet our old friend, Ernst Lachnit, but this time he is actually working in England, and quite successfully too. And through Ernst's experience we also come into contact with those typical mistakes. These episodes in Ernst's life are light and humorous.

In the chapters you will find:

The Storyboard: A text with dialogue built-in describing the adventures of Ernst. In the text his mistakes are indicated by a raised number (okay, treasure[1]). Look at the footnote at the bottom of the page for the correct form. There is an appendix to the footnotes with more explanations.

Laughing at Grammar: Two or three exercises covering tenses, if-sentences, tags etc. It's all based on jokes.

Crossing cultures: Extra information on the subject to give an idea about what's going on in Britain.

Laughing a little: A couple of jokes on the topic. No exercise! Just smile!

Perfect your phrasals: A short list of phrasals and idioms to help to build up a little dictionary of everyday language. Ernst also has a lot of trouble with these things. One base verb is dealt with in each chapter. The base verb appears in the storyboard.

Cultural quiz for brainwares: A set of general questions on Britain.

Playing with words: Two or three exercises to practise the new language items the chapter.

Tip of the day: Things to think about when going to Britain.

There is an **appendix of notes to the footnotes** for extra information. A key with answers and suggestions for all exercises appears at the end. And last but not least, a dictionary of English to German where all difficult words or phrases appear.

I hope you will enjoy Ernst and his new career in Britain.

Good luck!
René Bosewitz

LOVE'S PULL

1 A year has passed and Ernst Lachnit and Jenny got the "hots" for each other. Ernst has become something of an international "animal". He's always on the move, travelling on business when he can. But in his back head[1] is the idea to get to the UK permanently. You can guess why. And then as from the merry sky[2] his chance came. Ernst had the possibility to transfer to the UK. His company has a branch in Hampstead in London, and he landed the job. It's a three-year contract. "Where's the handy[3]? I've got to discuss this with Jenny."

1 at the back of his mind 2 completely out of the blue 3 mobile phone, cell or cellular phone

LAUGHING A LITTLE

Jenny: Do you really love me, or do you only think you do?
Ernst: Sweetheart, I really love you. I haven't done any thinking yet.

Love may be blind, but it seems to be able
to find its way round in the dark.

LAUGHING at GRAMMAR

Help the words in ( ).

a) A tourist was __________(ask) what he thought about warm English beer. He __________(reply), "I think they ought to pour it back into the horse."

b) Ernst went for a weekend trip to Cornwall, a county in the south-west of England. He stopped to talk to a farmer.
Ernst: Hi, do you __________(farm) around here?
Farmer: Aye.
Ernst: It's a beautiful day, isn't it?
Farmer: Aye.
Ernst: Have you __________ (live) here all your life?
Farmer: Not yet.

c) Fritz was __________(charge) with stealing a Mercedes, and after a long trial the jury __________(acquit) him. Two days later Fritz __________ (go) back to the judge. "Your Honour," he said, "I want __________(get) out a warrant for that lousy lawyer of mine."
"Why?" asked the judge. "He __________ (win) your case. Why do you __________ (want) him arrested?"
"Well, your Honour, I didn't have the money to pay him, so he went and took the car I stole."

1

C CROSSING CULTURES

Getting to know the British

Perhaps the first thing Ernst will notice when he begins to move around in Britain is the variety of people. Even in England itself there are differences between the smooth southerner and the dour northerner, then we have the talkative Welsh and the cantankerous Scots. There are many sub-groups in the picture, too; possibly the best known internationally is the famous, rather cold Englishman with his stiff upper lip and the notorious football hooligan with his shaven head. All of them are part of the same melting pot that enjoys the title "British".

The English

These people are a mixture of contradictions. It's difficult to know exactly what they mean. When they are being most polite, it probably means they are laughing at somebody. Nothing is quite as it seems. Back to the contradictions.

Marriage: we use this institution more frequently than any other European nation, but we have almost the highest divorce rate.

Work: on average we work more than any other European Union country (43.9 hours per week), but our productivity is the lowest.

Family life: is always promoted and emphasised, yet many well-heeled English families send their children off to boarding school as soon as they can.

Behaviour: we are famous for our tolerance and fair play, but seem to accept a divisive class system even in the year 2000. We can be over-polite, but at the same time extremely rude, disrespectful and biting.

And what about the Welsh?

For us English the Welsh seem to be a more compact group. We see them as warm-hearted, garrulous, more emotional. Wales has worked hard for centuries to protect its individuality and culture from its English "big brother".

Actually Wales is not as compact and homogenous as it first seems. In North Wales the Welsh language is still spoken, people there tend to look down upon their southern brothers whose blood is much more mixed. Northerners consider them as being anglicised.

A few words about the Scots

Some English see the Scots as dour and uncommunicative. That's probably because a lot of Scots don't want to talk to what they see as typical Englishmen. They, the Scots, or some of them at least, feel they have been robbed and dominated by London. In some ways they have never been integrated into Britain; they were never conquered by the Romans and they weren't centralised after 1066 by the Normans. In 1996 they voted to set up their own parliament in Edinburgh.

LAUGHING A LITTLE

The Englishman

An American visitor to England was a passenger on a train and, starting a conversation with an Englishman who was in his compartment, he said: "Do you know that you can board a train in Texas and after travelling for 24 hours you'd still be in Texas?"
The Englishman replied, "yes, I know. We've got trains like that in England, too."

The Welsh

Found in a Welsh newspaper. Excuses written down on their claim forms following car accidents:

- Coming home I drove into the wrong house and hit a tree I don't have.
- I collided with a stationary bus coming the other way.
- A pedestrian hit me and went under my car.
- The pedestrian had no idea which way to go, so I ran over him.
- In my attempt to kill a fly, I drove into a telegraph pole.

LAUGHING A LITTLE

The Scot

In spite of the long line behind him, the Scotsman at the Radio City Musical Hall box office counted his change very carefully, three times. The ticket seller watched him for a while and finally grew impatient, "What's the matter?" he asked. "Isn't the change right?"
"Oh, it's right," the Scotsman said, "but only just."

PERFECT your PHRASALS

Ernst had some problems to find the right phrasal or idiom. So he's decided to create his own dictionary. It's not only Ernst's problem, by the way.

➜ Ernst was *getting the hots* for Jenny. (Er war scharf auf Jenny.)

GET

get the sack/boot	entlassen werden
get into hot water	Ärger bekommen
get too big for one's boots	eingebildet werden
get up to something	etwas anstellen
get out of it	erlassen bekommen, davonkommen
get off	davonkommen
get on with	zurechtkommen mit

LAUGHING A LITTLE

The school we all know

Teacher: All right, you boys! Sit down and be quiet! What a mess this classroom is! What did you get up to in the last lesson?

Ernst: We didn't do anything, sir. It was the other class that left everything like that.

Teacher: Now, don't try to get out of it! I know it was you. I was watching you through the window. You're not going to get off that way.

Ernst: Oh, sir! We were all getting on so well together. And now "big brother" is watching us.

CULTURAL QUIZ for BRAINWARES

1. A little geography. Can you name the capital cities of
   a) Scotland b) Wales c) Northern Ireland?
2. Which city was the birthplace of Britain's most famous pop-group, the Beatles?
   a) Manchester b) Doncaster c) Liverpool
3. Which country in Britain is generally said to have the most talkative people?
4. Where might you see men wearing skirt-like clothing and what is it called?
5. Which famous English woman had her 100th birthday in 2000?
6. Where is the Celtic language still spoken?
7. Which was the only battle that the English actually lost and when did it take place?
8. Name the three counties that make up the West country.
9. Which mountain range is called the backbone of England?
10. What's the name of the famous apple drink that comes from Somerset in England?

PLAYING with WORDS

Find the English for the following simple sentences.

1. Ernst kam spät nach Hause und sah ziemlich belämmert aus. "Was hast du denn angestellt?", wollte Jenny wissen.
2. Seit Ernst seinen neuen Job hat, ist er eingebildet.
3. Der Polizist stoppte Ernst wegen zu schnellen Fahrens, aber weil er Ausländer war, kam er noch mal davon.
4. Jenny und Ernst verdienten nicht genug, deshalb bekamen sie Ärger mit ihrer Bank wegen der Hypothek.

TIP of the day

You can buy the cheapest trips in the Internet. And you've got a lot of choice. It's good to drive, ferry with P&O from Calais to Dover, then you're only 20 minutes from Canterbury.

2

Full of excitement Ernst phones the love of his life to impart the good news. But other feelings were rising, too. Ernst has to learn to be patient. We see how easy it is to get into an argument when you can't see who you're talking to.

S THE STORYBOARD

The first thing Ernst wanted to do was phone Jenny with the great news. Our hero phoned her at work at the hospital. She wasn't there. Bad luck! Let's try her home number. No result! Well, where can she be? She should have been at work. Perhaps she's out with some other boy. Ernst suddenly felt hot all over. "Where is that girl ?" Suddenly the phone rang. It made him jump. Angrily he put the receiver to his mouth. "Yes." "It's me, Jenny. I've got a message to say you were looking for me."

"Yes, I was. Where were you? I tried your flat, the hospital." "We were in the operating theatre. You know, they won't disturb me there."

Ernst got himself under control. "Right. I see. Okay, treasure[1], do you want the good news or the bad?"

"Ernst, can't you be normal on the phone? I really look forward to your calls, but you always seem to make them more difficult."

Ernst felt defensive. "Now, now, don't take it all so earnst[2]. After all, I'm the only Ernst in your life, or at last[3] I hope so."

"That might be, but seven hundred miles is more than spitting distance."

"Do you want the news, or not?"

Jenny was getting frustrated. "Go on, stop wasting my money!"

"The good news is that I can transfer to England. I can join you. And I'll even be paid for the pleasure."

Jenny tried to hide her surprise. "Wow, that's a bit ... That's a surprise."

"Surprise? It's great news. The bad news is that I'll be in Hampstead, North London. That's hundred miles from Canterbury."

A little provoked, Jenny, "well, it's a lot better than the present situation. We could see each other every weekend or second weekend."

Ernst was definitely feeling annoyed. This long distance relationship had certainly put pressure on everybody's nerves. "Frankly spoken[4] I'm somewhat tired of all this. What I need is something more stable. To give us a chance. Everything else is very stressful. I'll phone you later."

1 sweetheart, darling 2 seriously 3 at least 4 to be frank

2 LAUGHING at GRAMMAR

Let's check our verb tenses!

a) Ernst is on the way to England.
Ernst approached the ticket counter at British Airwegs and ________ (ask) for a reservation from Frankfurt to London. The clerk ________ (know) that the plane ______ (be) very full with luggage and passengers. "How much you _______ (weigh), sir?" asked the clerk. "With or without clothes?" Ernst wanted to know. "Well," ________ (say) the clerk, "how do you intend to travel?"

b) When Ernst arrived at the frontier, he had the following dialogue:

Passport Control:	________ (Have) you any money in the bank?
Ernst:	Certainly.
Passport Control:	How much?
Ernst:	I don't know. I _________ (not shake) it lately.

c) Ernst: Every time I _________ (have) a cup of coffee, I get a stabbing pain in my right eye. What shall I ________ (do)?
Jenny: _______ (Take) the spoon out of your cup.

C CROSSING CULTURES

Mentalities

You may have noticed in the telephone conversation between Ernst and Jenny that all was not well. Now what's that all about? Fact is it's about the question of mentality.

Ernst, our German boy, has new information. He wants to communicate it immediately. He needs to be direct. But he forgets at the same time that Jenny also has another way of life. She's a Brit. She's muddling through and living for today. Jenny doesn't make plans because she belongs to a society which thinks that even the best-laid plans will go wrong.

We Brits prefer to relax and enjoy life and work within our natural boundaries. Things should not be over-organised. Actually, the thinking of many people in Britain is "well, we can't win anyway", or "he's not well-suited to business" or "you're not the right type for that sort of job, but never mind". Compare that to the German feeling. It's not the same.

Ernst was already beginning to arrange, to create a schedule, to plan for the future. But as a Brit Jenny hates too much bustle (no hectic); she doesn't want to change the course of her life. Typical Brits don't even like to sign contracts for a rented apartment. It's all too permanent. Brits have a great capacity for contentment and can be happy with small successes. They feel it's not worth getting upset about the future. Compare German thinking!
As a group the Brits are a bit chaotic. It's a particularly British attitude to muddle through.

All this is the background to our phone-call. Ernst had achieved his target, but not discussed the matter with Jenny. She, on the other hand, was suddenly forced to make decisions, to change her life.
What's the bottom line? Open your eyes to others, think about your behaviour, climb out of your own back garden and be ready to make compromises.
Good luck, Jenny! Good luck, Ernst!

2 LAUGHING A LITTLE

Ernst asked his close friend in Heidelberg for advice.

Ernst: Could I ask your advice on a rather important matter, my old school friend?

Robert: Certainly.

Ernst: Well, it's like this. I'm in love with two girls. One is very beautiful but she's poor. The other is pleasant but plain, and she's got a pile of money. What would you do in the circumstances?

Robert: I'm sure in your heart you love the beautiful one, so I'd go ahead and marry her.

Ernst: Okay. That's what I'll do.
(Robert was on his way out)

Robert: Oh, by the way, I wonder if you could give me the phone number of the other girl?

"Will you marry me?" asked Ernst, getting down on his knees and offering Jenny a glittering ring.
"Oooh," she exclaimed, "are they real diamonds?"
"I hope so," said Ernst proudly. "Because if they aren't, I've been swindled out of ten pounds."

PERFECT your PHRASALS

Of course, Ernst's old problem goes on. Here are a few more.

FEEL

feel up to something	sich zutrauen
feel for	mitfühlen mit
feel like a fish out of water	sich deplatziert vorkommen
feel under the weather	gesundheitlich nicht gut gehen
feel out of sorts	nicht auf dem Damm sein

LAUGHING A LITTLE

Best test

Ernst: I hate driving in foreign countries. I feel like a fish out of water as soon as I see foreign signs everywhere. It makes me nervous and I get a headache.

Jenny: Just take it easy. There's nothing to worry about. You're feeling out of sorts because the weather's so hot. We're in the south, after all.

Ernst: Listen, Jenny, could you drive? It'd be safer.

Jenny: That's true enough! By the way, where did you pass your driving test?

Ernst: Well, in the Odenwald, but we don't have any foreign drivers there. It's easier.

2 CULTURAL QUIZ for BRAINWARES

1. Which company is the main supplier of telephones in the U.K.?

2. Newspapers! Let's say there are the "heavies" (with a lot of information), and the boulevard press (more pictures and football). Which paper belongs in which category? B or H (boulevard or heavy)?
   a) The Sun b) The Observer c) The Daily Express
   d) The Telegraph e) The Guardian f) The Times
   g) The Mirror h) The Evening Standard

3. TV! How many national terrestrial channels are there in Britain?
   a) four b) five c) six

4. What is the most popular spectator and participant sport?

5. Still on sport. Early in the 19th Century a young pupil picked up the ball and ran with it. This marked the beginning of which famous sport?

6. Even more on sport! Fill in the gaps.
   a) Ernst plays golf on a ________ ________.
   b) He broke his leg playing football on a football ________.
   c) Jenny prefers to spend her time on the tennis ________.
   d) Michael Shoemaker races round the motor-racing ___________ at top speed.

7. How many deutschmarks are there in a pound (approximately)?

8. There's a famous circle of stone in the south of England which was used for religious purposes. What's its name? St__________.

9. What's the Union Jack?

10. On the road. What's the speed limit in towns?
    a) 25 miles per hour b) 30 c) 40
    and outside towns
    a) 60 miles per hour b) 50 c) 45

PLAYING with WORDS

Ernst is still having trouble with these phrases. Help him!

1. Our Ernst drank a whole bottle of wine the day of the phone-call with Jenny. Next day he had a bad head and didn't feel ______ ______ doing anything.
2. After he arrived at his new job in London he was lost. He didn't understand the processes, the humour, or the language properly. Ernst felt like a ______ ______ ____ water.
3. "I'd better start doing a good job, or I might even get _______ ______," thought Ernst after his first week of work.

TIP of the day

If you're staying in a town get the local evening newspaper to find out what's going on. There you'll find cinema, TV, radio and clubs.

3

In this episode Ernst, frustrated and eager to confront Jenny, phones her up again. A fiery conversation follows and a lot of wasted words. In addition hear something about Brits abroad.

S THE STORYBOARD

An hour later Jenny phoned Ernst again: "Why didn't you phone back?"

"I wasn't ready to."

"Oh, I see. Well, what exactly did you mean? What were you getting at?"

Ernst felt better. At least she had heard what he was saying. "Okay, I think it's highest time that we live[1] together. Now we've got the chance. Let's pack it[2]!"

Jenny was confused. "What do you mean! Pack it. So you want to stop the relationship?"

"Nonsense[3]. I said we should grab the bull by the balls."

Laughing Jenny informed Ernst that he had used the wrong idiom. "I think you mean 'grab the bull by the horns'. You've picked up the wrong words from those English teachers of yours. But seriously, what about my job? Remember, I'm a nurse. I've got responsibilities."

"We've all got responsibilities. Not only you." Somehow he was getting sensitive again. Was she trying to avoid him? He didn't feel quite happy. Her cross voice whistled in his ear. "Ernst, you're being selfish. You come over here and think everything's got to change. It's not fair."

Ernst, by now angry, "Oh, that had just failed me[4]. We have a chance and you just don't want to see it. A big mouth and nothing behind it[5]." That was too much for Jenny. "How dare you? You've no understanding. Good-bye!" She bangs the phone down. One hour later the phone rings again. "Hello, Lachnit." Jenny's voice was at the other end. "Okay, but be it on your own head. I've got a chance to move to Hampstead Hospital and I'll take it. I'll take the bull by the horns." Ernst was over the moon. "Yeahhh."

---

1 It's high time that we lived ...
2 Let's get down to it / let's get on with it / let's take the bull by the horns. "Pack it" often means "stop it".
3 Not at all / of course not. Nonsense is too strong, even rude.
4 Oh, that was all I needed.
5 You're all talk.

3 LAUGHING at GRAMMAR

Help the words in ( ).

a) _______ (hear) you about the man from the income-tax office who _______ (phone) a certain Baptist minister to say, "we _______ (check) the tax returns of a member of your church, Deacon Hahn? We _______ (notice) he lists a donation to your building fund of £700. Is that correct?" The minister _______ (answer) without hesitation, "I _______ (not have) any records available, but I promise you one thing: If he _______ (not have), he will!"

b) Ernst was in the barber's shop. A good-looking girl _______ (give) a manicure to another customer. Ernst lay back in his chair. "How about a date later?" he _______ (ask) "I _______ (be) married," she said. "So _______ (call) up your husband and _______ (tell) him you're going to visit a girlfriend." She said, "you _______ (tell) him yourself. He _______ (shave) you."

c) Jenny: My boyfriend is no good.
Jean: But I thought you _______ (tell) me last week that he _______ (be) a model boyfriend.
Jenny: He is a model boyfriend – but not a working model.

C CROSSING CULTURES

The Brits away from home

Nowadays, a lot of people from the island can afford to go on holiday twice a year. Well, you've certainly got Brits who visit a foreign country to find out about its culture, local food, history and architecture. But perhaps this is a dying breed. More often we can spy the package holiday-maker. These people get cheap all-inclusive holidays in certain places like the south of Spain, Costa del Sol, Terremolinas, the Algarve in Portugal, and the famous Ibiza.

Very often they hang around the hotel swimming pools or discos in groups. These young Brits certainly let their hair down, a process which already begins in the aeroplane. Here, they indulge in their favourite pastime of swilling back the alcohol rapidly and indiscriminately. By the time they reach the hotel they are inebriated, referred in the common language as "pissed as a newt" or "under the table" or "bladdered".

So much for the drinking habits of the Brit abroad. This skill of getting violently drunk (also a consequence of the alcohol being so cheap in comparison with the UK) is famous. There are instances of Brits running around throwing chairs through windows and attacking people, especially, if there is a football match in the area.

These lively representatives of British culture do their best to plant it on foreign lands. So, everywhere we find groups of Brits, we will also recognise cafés that offer the eternal baked beans, egg and bacon, fish and chips and warm beer which is an attempt to create indigestion and heart-burn. Perhaps I should mention that stereotypes can bee seen all over the place. I'm sure if we think hard enough we can find another country with similar citizens. Replace Fish & Chips by Frankfurters and Sauerkraut or pig's legs, and Ibiza by Majorca and we have it.

But in the end it's all very healthy. Resting in the sun with a hangover until all skins are "as red as a beetroot" and skin cancer is only a few cells away.

I'm looking forward to my next vacation. What about you?

3

LAUGHING A LITTLE

Hotel receptionist in Spain to Englishman: "Are you a foreigner?"
Englishman: "Certainly not! I'm British!"

Resident of Barbados: "In Barbados we always have fantastic weather."
Visiting English woman: "Then how on earth do you start a conversation with a stranger?"

A holiday is something you have for two weeks
that takes fifty weeks to pay for.

The last time I went on holiday for a fortnight it only rained twice.
The first time for seven days, and the second time for a week.

It was on a sightseeing coach tour of New York that the Welshman turned to his companion, a boastful American, and said: "And where do you come from?" "From God's own country," replied the American. "Hmm," said the Welshman, "then you've got a very poor Welsh accent!"

Ernst, who was in Scotland, had been admiring the scenery. He stopped as he passed through a village and asked one of the inhabitants. "Is this a healthy place?" "Aye, it is," came the reply. "There's been only one death in the last ten years, and that was the local undertaker who died of starvation."

Jenny: Do you love me with all your heart and soul?
Ernst: Yes, I do.
Jenny: Do you think I'm the most beautiful girl in the world?
Ernst: Uh-huh.
Jenny: Do you think my lips are like rose petals?
Ernst: Uh-huh.
Jenny: Oh, you say the most beautiful things.

PERFECT your PHRASALS

We read in the hot line that Ernst had picked up the wrong words in English.

PICK

pick up	aufgabeln, mit dem Auto abholen
pick on (somebody)	hänseln, herumhacken auf
pick out	ausmachen, auswählen
pick up speed	schneller fahren
pick a quarrel	einen Streit anfangen
pick holes (in)	an jemandem herumkritisieren

LAUGHING A LITTLE

Road hog

Jenny: Ernst, I know you're the driver, but I really must tell you that you've been gradually picking up speed again. You're driving too fast.

Ernst: Well, you're right. I am the driver of this vehicle and I'll drive as fast as I want. So don't try to pick a quarrel with me.

Jenny: Ok, but you always pick holes in my driving.

Ernst: That's different. You're a woman and you don't understand machinery or cars.

Jenny: Well, you're a man and you're a male chauvinist pig, as well. You're not such a great driver, either.

Ernst: I'm always in full control of the vehicle.

Jenny: Then, why is that police car signalling to you?

Ernst: He's probably lost his way.

Policeman: Sir, you were driving too fast and without due care and attention. Have you passed your driving test?

3

CULTURAL QUIZ for BRAINWARES

1. Can you name at least three airports located in London?
2. Which Iron Lady initiated the building of the Channel Tunnel?
3. What on earth is a double-decker? Hint, it's not a hamburger!
4. In your opinion, what's the most popular meal that many Brits queue up for on Fridays (and other days, too)?
5. What's the name of a spicy food eaten with rice that's also available as a takeaway all over Britain?
6. What is the largest ethnic community in Britain?
7. In England people sometimes have afternoon tea. What does this meal consist of?
8. Since we're talking about food, exactly what is the following: Wensleydale / Gloucester / Stilton / Cheshire / Cheddar?
9. When you're touring around in England you can stay overnight at a private house and eat breakfast in the morning. What's this type of accommodation called?
10. Finally, the word "toast" has two meanings. One is a piece of bread burnt brown for your breakfast, but what do we mean when we "toast" a person getting married?

PLAYING with WORDS

a) Translate the following text!

Ernst: Okay. Fangen wir an! Wir müssen über meinen Umzug nach England reden, hab ich Recht?

Mutter: Ich glaube, es wird dir gut tun. Es ist allerhöchste Eisenbahn, dass du auf eigenen Beinen stehst. Du redest immer vom Reisen, aber du tust nie etwas.

Ernst: Das ist genau, was ich gebraucht habe. Vielen Dank für deine Unterstützung. Willst du einen Streit anfangen? Ich bin gekommen, um dich um Rat zu fragen.

Mutter: Natürlich, mein lieber Junge. Achtung, sei vorsichtig! Du wirst schneller. Du befindest dich in einem Wohngebiet.

b) Ernst has forgotten his words. Can you help him?

1. Clerk: So you want to cancel your ferry ticket?
Ernst: (Quatsch) __________. I just want to go a week later.

2. Ernst told his mother, "When I go to England I'll be a (Vertreter) ______________ of our German culture."

3. "Jenny, when I arrive could you (abholen) _________ me from the airport?"

4. Ernst again to his mother, "I really can't understand why you (herumkritisieren) _______________ in me the whole time. You'd think I was a complete failure."

TIP of the day

You can still get cheap flights and cheap holidays by booking through Britain. You can get good language courses in Britain nowadays too.

4

In this chapter Ernst begins to make some friends in the UK. He has to indulge in some small talk, which is not so easy. Ernst normally prefers to talk about serious topics.
We also get a short overview of English humour which is already well represented all over the world.

S THE STORYBOARD

So the important decision was made. Ernst "Laughalot" packed his few belongings together, bought a ticket to London by train, said his good-byes to everybody and was off. The first part of his journey was comfortable. "I really like travelling in this ICE." But the rest wasn't so good. No restaurant car, hardly a drink and full. But eventually he arrived in London. Jenny picked him up from St. Pancras Station and drove him to a friend's apartment in the north of London. "We can stay here for a week or two. And in the meanwhile we could visit some estate agents and check out a few flats."

The happy couple had a small room at Jane Johnson's place. Jane was a former nursing colleague of Jenny's. That evening, in front of an open fire Jenny, Ernst, Jane and her boyfriend from Scotland, Ian were getting to know each other. The typical small talk opened up. They were already down the first half bottle of Burgundy.

Ian, in a lively voice. "So, you arrived this morning, Ernst ? What are your first impressions?"

Ernst thought for a minute. "Well, I'm a bit shocked. The informations[1] I had in Germany were that England is a cheap country." Ian laughed. "Your news media are out of date. Everything has become expensive here. Even the beer."

"Yes, I know. Last year I made a course[2] here in England. Prices are much higher than then." Jenny agreed with Ernst. "Yes, and on top of that there's the problem of the exchange rate. Ernst felt in control of things. After all, business and economics was his thing." "Yes, the pound has gained about twenty-five percent against the Euro and the Deutschmark. I think we did a mistake[3] when we started so quickly with the Euro." Jane was surprised. As she threw another log onto the fire she looked closely at Ernst. "I thought most Germans were in favour of it?" "Probably they are, but I have difficulties to accept it[4]. I think that everything was done in a hurry as usual. It seems to be typical for[5] all our governments and leaders."

1 information
2 I did a course
3 made a mistake
4 I have a problem to accept it / I have difficulties in accepting it
5 typical of

4 "You might be right there," Ian chipped in loudly. "It was the same with our Scottish parliament." "Oh, not that again. I've heard this story a hundred times. Ernst, tell us, have you had the pleasure of our English cuisine?" "Oh dear me," interrupted the ever patient Jenny. "This could be a long evening."

LAUGHING at GRAMMAR

Same again. Fill in the correct forms.

a) It was a ___________ (langweilig) Sunday afternoon in the jungle so the elephants decided ___________ (challenge) the ants to a game of soccer. The game ___________ (go) with the elephants ___________ (beat) the ants ten goals to nil, when the ants got the ball. The ants' star player ___________ (dribble) the ball towards the elephants' goal when the elephants' left-back came ___________ (lumber) towards him. The elephant trod on the little ant ___________ (kill) him immediately. The referee stopped the game. "What the devil do you think you're doing? Do you think that's fair, ___________ (kill) another player? The elephant replied, "well, I didn't mean ___________ (kill) him. I was trying ___________ (trip) him up."

b) How many Englishmen does it take ___________(change) a light bulb? What do you mean ___________(change) it? It's a perfectly good light bulb! We've had it for 100 years and it's worked just fine.

C CROSSING CULTURES

The island humour

It's often said of the Brits that they have a black sense of humour. Black in this case really means that they laugh in situations causing pain to others. As with most things in life it's not as easy as that.

Generally in Britain, if you want to be funny you have to portray yourself as being a loser and a bit of a fool. You are not in line with the rest of society, you're out of time. An example of this is John Cleese as Basil Fawlty in Fawlty Towers. Other comedians who were out of line include Morecambe & Wise or the Two Ronnies. Most of you have encountered Monty Python's Flying Circus which is on the edge of madness and very much out of line, it might be said. I'm sure we all know the various adventures of Mr Bean who doesn't speak, but rather mimes and exaggerates the various feelings that he experiences while spinning through life. Whether sitting on a park bench eating a live fish or stuffing the Christmas turkey and getting it stuck on his head, Mr Bean addresses us all with strong pathos.

Death is a topic which often appears in English humour. Brits find it hugely funny to talk about death in its many forms.

"Buried the cat last week."
"Did it die, then?"
"No, we just didn't like it very much."
or
Doctor: "You're in great shape. You'll probably reach 90."
Patient: "I am 90."
Doctor: "Oh, well. That's it, then."

For the more academic ones among you, there are more or less five categories of humour:

Irony: it's a form of self-mockery. It's a virtue to laugh at oneself.

Satire: the ability to laugh at national habits & institutions. Examples of this type of humour are 'Yes, Prime Minister' or 'Spitting Images'.

Smut: includes farces about sex, with people running around losing their trousers and like Benny Hill dressing up in women's clothes. It says something about the British attitude to sex.

Absurdity: with a lot of cruelty and sadism in this form. Earlier examples were the 'Goon Shows' and 'Monty Python'.

Wit: clever statements by famous people, including much of the work of William Shakespeare. A famous example from a discussion in the House of Parliament:

> Lady Aster told Winston Churchill, "If the Right Honourable Gentleman were my husband, I'd put poison in his tea."
> To which Churchill replied, "If the Right Honourable Lady were my wife, I'd drink it."

LAUGHING A LITTLE

The young girl was complaining to one of her friends:
"It was terrible! I had to change my seat five times
at the cinema last night."
"Why?" asked her friend. "Did some chap bother you?"
"Yes – eventually."

Men always say the most important thing in a woman is the sense of humour. You know what that means? He's looking for someone to laugh at his jokes.

A man went for a brain transplant and was offered the choice of two brains – an architect's for £ 10,000 and a politician's for £ 100,000.
"Does that mean that the politician's brain is much better than the architect's?" asked the man.
"Not exactly," replied the brain transplant salesman. "The politician's has never been used."

A friend is a guy who's got the same enemies as you do.

A beggar walks up to a well-dressed woman who is shopping in Oxford. "Mrs, I haven't eaten a thing for over a week." The wealthy lady looked at him with wonder and smiled. "My goodness, I wish I had your will-power."

Jenny (angrily): What do you mean by coming home half drunk?
Ernst: It's not my fault. I ran out of money.

I've never been on speaking terms with her. Listening terms, yes, but speaking terms, no!

PERFECT your PHRASALS

Now what's Ernst's problem phrasal this time? It's

PACK

pack in	aufhören
pack off	fortschicken
pack up	zusammenpacken / Schluss machen

LAUGHING A LITTLE

The customer is not always right!

Hotel manager:	Well, sir, you'd better pack up all your belongings and get out. We've had far too much trouble from you. A table and several glasses are broken.
Rude customer:	Hey, pack that in! What are you accusing me of? I've not broken anything.
Hotel manager:	Oh, there were other people living in this room with you, were there?
Rude customer:	The room had to be cleaned, didn't it? Perhaps it was the cleaning girl.
Hotel manager:	I think you'd better get out before I send for the police. They'll soon pack you off.

CULTURAL QUIZ for BRAINWARES

1. Do you remember the name of the Scottish loch where the monster lives?
2. Speaking of lakes, can you name two of the lakes in the English Lake District?
3. Can you name a famous film or TV series starring John Cleese?
4. Another famous British film star who is now dead was Peter Sellers. Do you know which series of films he made?
5. Who is supposed to have said "sport is death"?
6. On the historical side, do you know who fought in the War of the Roses?
7. How many wives did Henry VIII have? What happened to the ladies?
8. In the English political scene, who are the Tories?
9. London caught fire, called the Great Fire of London. When was that?
10. What is the BBC and what do the letters stand for?

PLAYING with WORDS

a) Ernst has forgotten some words. Can you fill them into his sentences?

1. Jenny, can you help me ______ ______ my suitcase? I haven't got much time.
2. The boss called me into his office because I ________ a stupid mistake with a customer.
3. Ernst got into an argument with a man in a pub. "It was absolutely typical ________ some of these over-patriotic fellows," complained Ernst.

b) Can you translate the following dialogue into English?

Mutter: Ernst, erhebe nicht deine Stimme gegen mich.

Ernst: Komm schon, lass uns aufhören zu streiten. Das ist es nicht wert!

Mutter: Du gehst nur wegen diesem Mädchen nach England und nicht wegen der Arbeit. Du kannst mir glauben, sie schickt dich fort, wenn du sie langweilst. Und dann bist du auf dich allein gestellt.

Ernst: Vielen Dank für deine Unterstützung, Mutter.

TIP of the day

Humour across borders can be difficult. Don't be ironic to people. It will cause feelings of aggression. Watching sitcoms can help you to understand the humour.

5

Our heroes are taking steps to find somewhere to live in London. Here we see them doing what is necessary at the estate agents. Ernst is trying to adapt.
We also learn about the Englishman's attitude to home and garden.

S THE STORYBOARD

It was nice living at Jane's flat, but, well two's company, three's a crowd, as the old saying goes. "I think it's time we go[1] to the estate agent. Maybe we'll find ourselves a cosy little flat." Ernst was thinking out loud. One hour later the happy couple were walking through the door of a rather shabby-looking estate agents in Hampstead. Nevertheless, Ernst was impressed. "Look at all these photos on the wall. You can get an impression of the different sorts of places. That's superior than[2] our 'maklers' in Germany. And cheap, too, from what you were telling me."

"Can I help you two people?" A deep voice chimed from a tall thin person who had just entered from a small back room. He looked more like an undertaker. "Yes. Could you give us some advices[3]? We're looking for a flat." "I guessed it might be something like that since you've come into my imporium here. Okay, what's your price range and which area do you fancy?"

"Round here somewhere would do," said Jenny quietly. "Yes, we need to be in an environmental[4] friendly area, plenty of green, water and soil," laughed Ernst. "Oh you're interested in the environment, are you? Then perhaps I could find something for you behind the Heath. There's plenty of green and water there. I don't know about the soil. You're not gardeners, are you? Or some other sort of 'green people'?" Jenny was a little irritated. "Actually, we do think people should take care of the environment, for the sake of our children." "Oh, very social, if I may say so. What can you afford to pay?" Ernst felt it was his turn. "We were thinking to pay not more as[5] £ 500 per month." "How many rooms would you like?" "Rooms? I thought you would do it in square metres." "No, we don't calculate like that." Ernst thought a while. "Three rooms, bathroom and kitchen, I guess."

"Furnished?" was the next question. Jenny was quick to reply. "Unfurnished. We'd like to pick up our own furniture at auctions if we can." The undertaker smiled. An unexpected gesture from his side. "Yes, that's a good idea. There are some great antique shops around here, too.

1 we went 2 superior to 3 advice 4 environmentally friendly 5 more than

5 Look at this photograph. It's a ground floor flat with a small garden at the back. The owner wants £ 520 per month. It's standing empty at the moment. I can give you the key and you can drive over and have a look. Bring the key back when you've finished." Ernst was enthusiastic. "Great, it's all so easy. And what a beautiful weather today[6]! I've got a good feeling."

LAUGHING at GRAMMAR

Make your choice!

a) The young man ❒ walked / ❒ has walked into the pet shop and asked if he could buy 362 beetles, 35 rats and 5 mice. "I'm sorry, sir, but we can only supply the mice. But what ❒ are / ❒ were the other creatures needed for?" asked the pet shop manager. "I ❒ was / ❒ have been thrown out of my flat this morning," replied the young man. "And my landlord says it must ❒ be / ❒ being left exactly as it ❒ was / ❒ has been found."

b) Home is the place to stay while the car is ❒ being / ❒ been serviced.

c) Home is the place where, no matter where you're sitting, you're looking at something that needs to ❒ be / ❒ being done.

d) Ernst: Jenny, I'm not saying that that flat was scruffy but last year it ❒ was broken / ❒ was breaked into and ❒ decorated / ❒ decorating.

6 what beautiful weather

C CROSSING CULTURES

An Englishman's home

So, we all know the famous expression that "an Englishman's home is his castle". Just to make sure that the whole thing is well-understood and not misinterpreted this does not mean that it is a "castle" to keep strangers out, like a fortress. The opposite can be true, in fact. Friends can come around unannounced. No, it's rather meant in the way that these are my own four walls, and I can do what I like (within reason). And the English do a lot in their homes.

There is a whole cycle of home improvements, for which there are numerous loans and lines of credit from the major banks. No home can be a real home without these investments. Every corner has to have its extension, every attic must be converted.

As for the gardens. Well, an English country garden is a "must". You wouldn't believe it, but the TV is a witness to it. Every day on the five national TV channels there are a multitude of gardening and decoration programmes – maybe ten per day. They're all innovative and entertaining. Just imagine you went off for a romantic weekend, arrived back and found your dining room redesigned, or your garden had turned into a theme park.

Of course, the big thing in Britain is DIY. It stands for Do It Yourself! What it really means is hundreds of incompetent people run around huge DIY hypermarkets buying enough equipment to start a company, misuse the tools and eventually have to call in an expert to put it right. The experts come along, look sideways at the mess, and hiss between their teeth, "You've been fiddling with this, haven't you?"

Back to gardens! Some non-English persons might think football is the national sport. You've got it all in the wrong throat[7]. No, it's gardening and every little Englander thinks he's got green fingers. No, it's nothing to do with diseases like mad cows, crazy bulls and swinish pigs. It's all about "You can grow things. You're a grower!"

---

7 You've got the wrong end of the stick

Other people let their gardens grow. The island monkeys try to transplant everything with a green stem. Trees from Tibet, meat-eating orchids, tropical gardens and all that for a climate that's in permanent flood. Hmmm! To tell the truth they got it right in Xenophobe's guide to the English and I quote, "For the English the first sound of spring is not really the song of the cuckoo, but the echo of the unprintable oath of the gardener who discovers that his lawnmower will not start."

LAUGHING A LITTLE

A garden is a thing that dies if you don't water it
and rots if you do.

"What are you doing up my tree, young man?"
"Well, one of your apples fell down, and I'm putting it back."

What is a weed?
A plant whose virtues have not been discovered.

Ernst: Can I put this wallpaper on myself?
Jenny: Of course, you can, sweetheart, but it'll probably look better on the wall.

The only thing Ernst grows in the garden is tired.

Mad fools of gardeners go out in the pouring rain
To prove they're Anglo-Saxon
they rarely put their macks on;
Each puts on rubber boots and squelches through moist terrain,
Then leaves the mud and silt on
The Wilton [carpet].

Jenny: Why are you putting that evil-smelling green powder all over the garden?
Ernst: To keep crocodiles off it.
Jenny: But there aren't any crocodiles around here.
Ernst: See how good the green powder is.

PERFECT your PHRASALS

Can you help our Ernst? He's still not got it.

➜ Ernst was thinking out loud.

THINK

think over	überdenken
think to oneself	bei sich denken
think up	erfinden, sich ausdenken
think twice	es sich gut überlegen
think highly	viel halten von
think no end of	ungemein viel halten von
think it proper	es für richtig halten

LAUGHING A LITTLE

Grand visions

Ernst: Oh dear, I've just received my bank statement. It doesn't make good reading.

Jenny: Well, it's your own fault. You didn't think twice. You just bought that old Porsche. I must say I didn't think very highly of that idea from the very beginning.

Ernst: Come on. It wasn't like that. People here think no end of status symbols like motor cars. It shows that you are a successful person.

Jenny: But I don't think it proper for a representative to arrive at a company driving a big sports car. Your customers will think you buy luxuries with their money.

Ernst: Never mind, it's reliable.

Jenny: It's as old as you and just as reliable. It starts well, but it can't keep going.

5 CULTURAL QUIZ for BRAINWARES

1. The question of renting a house. You want a Reihenhaus. Which is it?
   a) semi-detached b) terraced c) detached

2. Who do you go to in order to find out about renting accommodation?
   a) flat share b) house share c) estate agent

3. What's the expression that tells us that you're a good gardener, you can grow things?
   You've got _________ ________.

4. What does DIY stand for?

5. Which is longer, three metres or three yards? Exactly what is a meter in yards, feet and inches?

6. How many litres is a pint?

7. British people don't calculate cost of flats or houses in square metres. How do they do it?

8. What's the tradition known as high tea?

9. What does the famous greasy English breakfast consist of?

10. In Germany most people live in rented flats. What is the situation in Britain?
    a) rented flats b) owned flats
    c) owned houses d) rented houses

PLAYING with WORDS

Help Ernst to get through it!

1. Although Ernst ____________ (viel halten von) his mother, he does dislike her continually interferring in his life.

2. Mother: Ernst, there are a lot of problems involved in going to England, and especially if some woman is involved. Please ___________ (gut überlegen) before you take any risks.

3. Jenny: So what sort of flat or house do we want to rent?
   Ernst: I'm not sure yet. We'll have to get some ________ (Ratschläge).

4. Estate agent: Yes, and we have a small cottage which is up for rent.
   Ernst: Very interesting. And where _________ (sich befinden) this cottage?
   Agent: It was ________ (bauen) back in the fifteenth century in Hamstead.
   Ernst: My God, doesn't it need to be ____________ (renovieren)?

TIP of the day

If you're into gardening, watch the many gardening programmes on TV. Check the papers. There are a lot of gardening centres everywhere.

6

Ernst and Jenny find their dream home in a suburb of London. Here are a few reactions to it. Ernst is learning to cope with new situations. There's also information about apartments and housing in Britain and the housing market.

S THE STORYBOARD

Probably you all thought that the happy couple took the flat. Actually, they didn't. In the end they found it a bit too small. Then, a stroke of luck. Jenny's friend, Jane, had a friend who had an old sixteenth century cottage. She had landed a job abroad, in New Zealand, and was going away for at least three years. So Jenny and Ernst got first refusal. And it didn't break the bank, either. Only £ 560 per month. Some of the furniture was staying in, but a lot of it they'd have to get themselves. At the cottage with Lesley.

Ernst was impressed. "This is all amazingly old and antique. Look at this kitchen with this old cooker." "We call that a Rayburn," Lesley informed him. "Of course, that's not really old. It just looks like it." Ernst looked around the house. In every room were wooden beams and open fireplaces. The ceilings were very low, too. "You have a different system here in England. In Germany we are used to get[1] a flat with nothing in it. No kitchen[2], nothing." Jane was puzzled. "No kitchen? You must have a kitchen. Where do you do your cooking? " Jenny intervened. "I think Ernst means there are no kitchen utilities, no cookers, fridges, etc." "Yes, it's a real problem. In these days[3] it is very expensive to buy new equipment each time you change your flat." Jenny and Ernst made a tour of the cottage.

They were already beginning to get some ideas on how they wanted to furnish the place. "Next Saturday morning there's an auction where we can get some old stuff if we're lucky. Ernst nodded his head in agreement. "Yes indeed. We have to undertake steps[4] to make a plan of what we want." "Oh, Ernst, you and your lists and steps and organising." "Order must be[5], or we'll all run around and do[6] all our jobs and tasks three or four times. Anyway, what's[7] about the townworks[8]?" This time Jennybell was confused. "Townworks?" "Yes, energy etc." Now she'd got the message. "You mean gas, electricity, waste water, water etc.? I've

---

1 we are used to getting 2 not including kitchen furniture 3 nowadays 4 take steps to ...
5 you have to be properly organised 6 we'll all be running around and doing ...
7 what about 8 electricity, gas company

got the telephone number. I'll just phone and they'll send a form with a direct debit or a standing order. We sign and send it back and we're switched on." "Fine." Ernst hadn't expected it to be so simple. "Anyway, let's make a list of the furniture we need. On number sure[9]."

LAUGHING at GRAMMAR

Help Ernst with his brackets!

a) The premises are so delightfully extensive that two people might live together without ever ________________(see, hear or meet).

b) ___________ (keep) house is as unpleasant and filthy as coal mining, and the pay's a lot worse. *P.J. O'Rourke*

c) When we were finishing our house, we found we had a little cash left over, on account of the plumber not __________ (know) it.

9 to be on the safe side

C CROSSING CULTURES

Where to live

A bit about renting. If you're coming from abroad and probably won't be staying very long, a year or two, you'll have to rent. In the Greater London area you could get a two or three-bedroom flat for £ 200 a week, and that will have only basic amenities; don't expect a super-furnished or decorated flat.

Another possibility is to rent a house, though this can be expensive in London, the Home Counties, Oxford, Cambridge, Edinburgh etc. You're best to let your local estate agent deal with the landlord or you might get into trouble. And again, rented accommodation leaves a lot to be desired. There may be problems with rising damp, burst pipes and draughts from badly fitting doors. And, of course, most houses come with gardens and gardens need to be maintained or else you get into legal problems with the landlord. Of course, on the other hand, as mentioned before, gardening can be a great hobby and a good way into getting into real England.

In England, as in many other European countries, it is necessary to sign a contract so you should make sure it is clear who is responsible for what. When you have signed the contract it is almost impossible for the landlord to evict you until the period of stay expires.

Rents for houses vary depending on region. For example, a three-bedroom house in Wales may cost only £ 150 per week, whereas in London a small two-bedroom terrace could easily be £ 700 per week. Everybody wants to go to London – supply and demand.

Types of housing

Most British people live in a house as owner-occupiers, they have a mortgage from a bank or building society, buy the house and live in it themselves. In general we have terraced, semi-detached and detached houses. Terraced houses come in rows of five or ten houses joined together. Normally they come as "two or three up, two downs", i.e., two or three bedrooms upstairs, a dining room and living room downstairs. A bit more money and the family moves into a semi-detached. The idea is to finally acquire a detached house with its own garden. This is typical for the average family meaning one working parent, and one at home with two children. Of course, even this is changing under the pressure of living costs and consumerism.

Buying a house or flat

Most people are not rich. They need to arrange a mortgage from a bank or building society. These organisations will deal with all the bureaucracy. Some will expect you to have lived in Britain for a minimum of two years before they give you money. Others demand that you have permanent job. What's permanent on this earth?

LAUGHING A LITTLE

Buying a house

One of the mysteries of human conduct is why adult men and women are ready to sign documents which they do not read, at the behest of salesmen they do not know, binding them to pay for articles they do not really want, with money which they do not have.

Gerald Hurst

Ernst had to complain to the landlord about the walls being so thin. He said, "You've got to do something about my next-door neighbour's television." "You mean you can hear it?"
Ernst desperately, "No, I can see it."

Landlady: I've come to tell you that I'm going to raise the rent.
Ernst: Oh good, because I was just about to tell you that I can't.

The great advantage of a hotel is that it's a refuge from life.

Housewife (or girlfriend). You know – sleep-in maids.

PERFECT your PHRASALS

Ernst is still struggling with his phrases. It's really not so easy.
➜ And it didn't break the bank.

BREAK

break down	eine Panne haben
break off	eine Pause einlegen
break up	aufhören, zu Ende gehen
break a habit	eine Gewohnheit ablegen
break one's word	das Wort brechen

LAUGHING A LITTLE

A helpful hand

"This is the Radio One news: A dangerous criminal has broken out of prison and is thought to be in the area of Nottingham."

Jenny: Oh dear! That's here! What's the world coming to? Today somebody broke into our hospital.

Ernst: What did they steal?

Jenny: The designs for our hospital's latest service. We were all shocked. The director even decided to break off our departmental meeting. Anyway, did anything interesting happen to you today?

Ernst: Nothing much. My car broke down near the prison, actually. A friendly man in grey overalls repaired it for me. He asked me for a lift to the railway station. He borrowed my jacket, too. He said he worked at the prison.

Jenny: Well, I never did. Grey overalls. Hmmm!

6 CULTURAL QUIZ for BRAINWARES

1. I'm a twenty-three year-old bank clerk and I want to get a place. What might I typically afford?
   a) semi-detached b) terraced house c) three-bedroom apartment

2. I want to go on holiday to England for a week. What's the most popular form of accommodation?
   a) hotel b) hostel c) bed & breakfast

3. How do most English people offer their flats and houses on the market if they want to sell?

4. If you wanted to travel by car from the continent to Edinburgh in Scotland by the best route where would you take the ferry to?
   a) Hull b) Dover c) Southampton

5. Which monarch reigned the longest?

6. Land's End & John o'Groats! What is special about these two places?

7. Where might you eat haggis?

8. A terraced house! How many main rooms would that have typically?

9. A little bit of geography. What's the highest mountain in Wales, in Scotland, in Britain?

10. Remember Hadrian's Wall? Liar! What is it?

PLAYING with WORDS

Watch out for Ernst! Can you improve his English?

Ernst: Hi Jenny, what's about going to a disco this evening? I feel a bit lively.

Jenny: Oh, I don't know. I am on early shift tomorrow at the hospital.

Ernst: No fear! On number sure we can leave at eleven so we'll back to the cottage early.

Jenny: And then you'll want to go to the Indian takeaway. We'll be back after midnight.

Ernst: I know I'm used to eat late, but tonight I promise you, no late night snacks even though it is difficult to lay off a habit.

TIP of the day

Going to live in Britain?
Find the area you would prefer, visit it by car. Then go to the main street and find an estate agent. Find your price range. Check their Photos.

7

Ernst is getting into a bit of English life-style by visiting an auction. He wants to get furniture for their cottage. He quickly has to learn how to behave himself at such events.
In addition you get extra information on auctions, jumble sales and boot sales and the sorts of people who patronise them. Good luck, Ernst!

S THE STORYBOARD

The two young hopefuls moved into the cottage which was called Hampstead Hovel. (In the old days a hovel was a primitive place lived in by the poorest peasants.) There were a lot of things to be done. "Listen," said Jenny, "I'll phone the woodman, while you look through the newspaper for furniture auctions."

"Phone up the woodman? Why that[1]?" "Well, what would you like to burn in the open fires, petrol or something?"

Ernst was not amused. "Ha, ha. I had thought we could use coal, for example. Hmmph!" "No, my dear, the woodman delivers logs straight to the door." Ten minutes later it had all been arranged. In the meanwhile Ernst had found out that an auction was taking place the following Saturday afternoon.

Saturday afternoon in front of the auction hall:
"Jenny, you know at this time in Germany I would watch[2] football in the television[3]. I ..."

"Now just a minute. That's not what I want to hear. You're as much involved in furnishing this house as I am. It's my leisure time too, you know."

Ernst was shocked. "No, no, no. You've got it in the wrong throat[4]. I was only comparing."

Jenny relaxed a bit. "I hope so. It was a big change for me to come to London, you know. Back in Canterbury I had a peaceful life and my friends."

Ernst understood what she meant. London was a huge place. It needed a lot of time to travel from one part to another and it was loud and tiring. And all that travel cost a lot of money. It's true. You could walk from one side of Canterbury to the other in ten minutes. It was more or less the same in Heidelberg.

By now they were in the auction hall. They had walked around inspecting

1 what for? 2 I'd be watching 3 on television 4 you've got the wrong end of the stick

the goods and chose a beautiful oaken table and a pine kitchen cabinet that they were really interested in.

Suddenly the cabinet's turn came. The auctioneer began to speak. "And now to this charming pine kitchen cabinet. I'd like to begin at £ 150. Will anyone offer £ 160, £ 170, yes I see £ 180."

Ernst was getting nervous. He shouted out "I take it[5] for £ 200." The auctioneer ignored him. Jenny whispered in his ear." "Listen, in this auction you bid by raising your card with your number on it. You don't call out. Those are the rules."

By the time this information had been imparted to him the auctioneer's voice was floating loudly across the room. "Going, going, gone."

"Shit[6]," hissed Ernst. "I've missed it." "Calm down! We've got another chance with the table."

"And now I come to this wonderful oaken table." This time Ernst waited till the others were out. "Going, going ...," then Ernst raised his hand. His last competitor did not move. Ernst had won the table. "I'm not as silly as I appear[7]," he whispered happily to Jenny.

LAUGHING at GRAMMAR

Ernst is worried about his IF sentences. Help him!

a) If I _______ (have) my life to live over again, I'd live over a saloon bar.

b) You _________ (not be) drunk if you can lie on the floor without holding on.

c) I've got all the money I'll ever need if I ________ (die) by four o'clock this afternoon.

d) If a third of all the novelists and maybe two thirds of all the poets now writing __________ (drop) dead suddenly, the loss to literature would not be great.

5 I'll take it   6 Oh, damn!   7 I'm not that stupid after all

e) Dear Editor, what I have written is a damn good story. If you have any comments, ________ (write) them on the back of a cheque.

f) By all means marry; if you get a good wife, you ________ (become) happy; if you get a bad one, you ________ (become) a philosopher.

g) Our doctor would never really operate unless it ________ (be) absolutely necessary. He was just that way. If he __________ (not need) the money, he wouldn't lay a hand on you.

h) If it was raining soup, the Irish ________ (be) out with forks.

i) If you walk like a duck, and you quack like a duck, and you say you're a duck, you ________ (be) a duck. *George Bush*

j) I don't mind you smoking if you _________ (not mind) me being sick all over you.

C CROSSING CULTURES

A furnishing hobby

As we saw in the dialogue at the beginning of the chapter, the English cling to some strange old traditions. One of these is the visit to the auction or the antique fair to try to land a bargain. These bargains can be old vases, tables, cupboards and books that have degenerated almost into dust. In other countries in Europe people, when they have a house or apartment, go to furniture stores and buy equipment for a complete bedroom or kitchen. They'll spend anything up to £ 20,000 for this practical, if boring stuff. Some little Englanders do it too, but increasingly we find ourselves running off to the local auction or antique shops.

Of course, this group of people tend to be a little strange. They are the ones who live in old flats or country cottages. Country cottages are often up to five or six hundred years old. The booty captured from auctions and the like is lovingly transported back to the old sitting room with its big open fire and wooden beamed ceiling. These are the country cottages with the old cookers called hobs in the kitchen. In every room there are colours and perfumes from dried lavender and rose.

The items captured from the auctions and antique shops are normally not antique – they're just old and second hand. Occasionally, though, you can find just what you're looking for.

Boot sales

In many areas enterprising island monkeys have little sales of old things from their houses. They can be in the local church hall or simply in a field. Boot sales are small, but very interesting. The rear end of a car is called the boot in British English. The boot sale consists of all the things that have been lying around in the boot, or in the old attic or down below in the cellar. It's all good, clean fun!

By the way, these sort of people who sniff around after "old" things are frequently also the ones who grow those wonderfully wild cottage gardens spending their time browsing through garden and horticultural centres. It's all part of the British way of life.

Finally, the TV is the be all and end all in Britain as it is all over Europe. Why do I mention the telly here? Well, look into any list of TV programmes and you'll see two or three broadcasts on antiques and five or six on gardening and DIY programmes. Not to forget the many programmes on home-cooking. The latter is long overdue!

The jumble sale

All the local people bring along their old things which are going for a song. It's usually in the church hall on Saturday mornings. Actually, it's all about communication and networking. It's just an excuse to get together and chatter and drink tea and eat homemade cake.

LAUGHING A LITTLE

I once went to a jumble sale and bought a very old and very large bureau. While I was cleaning it I must have pressed a secret button because a large panel in the back of the bureau came open and three people fell out shouting: "Where am I? Where am I?" That's when I realised I had bought a "missing persons bureau".

Jenny: Did you know I collect antiques?
Jean: Yes, I've met your boyfriend, Ernst.

"I've prepared the turkey," said Ernst proudly to Jenny. "I've plucked it and stuffed it. All you have to do is kill it and cook it."

"Ernst, darling," exclaimed Jenny from the kitchen. "I'm afraid I've spoiled your breakfast. The eggs were frying nicely when all of a sudden the shells broke and it all became very messy."

PERFECT your PHRASALS

Ernst is still learning ...
➜ While you look through the newspaper.

LOOK

look forward to	sich freuen auf
look up	etwas in einem Buch nachschlagen
look after	betreuen
look a picture of health	blendend aussehen
look a sight	einen schrecklichen Anblick bieten
look the worse for wear	mitgenommen aussehen

LAUGHING A LITTLE

A Perfect Holiday

Jenny: Oh Ernst, we've had a really good holiday. O.k., it was a bit expensive, but now we can work hard again back home in England.

Ernst: Well, you certainly look a picture of health. You've had a real rest sunbathing all the time, eating olives and drinking red wine. You don't have any problems. But I look a real sight. I had to drive all the time, I'm completely tired out. For me it was no holiday.

Jenny: Don't exaggerate! You enjoyed your time with me. We got on well together. And what's a little bit of driving anyway? It was only 3000 kilometres.

Ernst: Yes, 3000 kilometres and it cost a hell of a lot of money. My bank account looks the worse for wear.

Jenny: What do you expect? You can't have a holiday for free.

Ernst: I think you've just had a holiday for free, haven't you?

Jenny: I don't know if I had a holiday for free, but I just spent three weeks with you. I can't say that was a holiday with you moaning all the time.

CULTURAL QUIZ for BRAINWARES

1. What do you usually bid for at an auction?
   a) houses b) furniture c) books
2. What does the auctioneer say at the end of the bids?
   a) going, going, gone! b) ready, ready, out c) all done, now!
3. Which tree is a symbol of Britain?
   a) holly b) pine-tree c) oak
4. What type of furniture is a cabinet?
5. What's the English for
   a) something captured and brought home
   b) pieces of wood holding up the ceiling

6. What's the name given to an old thing often having a high value?
7. Can you name three places where you might buy antiques?
8. When you go to an auction do you offer, bid or challenge?
9. Where are the following located?
   a) cellar **b)** attic **c)** boot
10. What is the flag of Britain?

PLAYING with WORDS

Ernst has forgotten some phrases and got some others wrong.

a) Arriving home

Jenny: Jesus, I'm completely tired out. I've had a lousy day at work.

Ernst: I can see that. You ________________ (bietest einen schrecklichen Anblick). What on earth happened? Did you have to _________ (betreuen) a difficult patient?

Jenny: That was part of it. And then there was a power failure twice. That didn't help matters.

Ernst: Yes, I heard something about that in the TV. (The doorbell rings.) Shit. That's the door. I get it. It's somebody from the hospital for you.

Jenny: Oh, not again!

b) What would you do with

1. a cabinet? **2.** some booty? **3.** an attic?
4. a bureau? **5.** a turkey?

TIP of the day

Don't waste time and money buying new things for the house. Go to antique shops or jumble sales. They are advertised in the local Friday Advertiser or second hand mag.

8

So Ernst is finding out some minor differences between German and English working practices. It's a bit shocking for him. And he begins to see the mixture of social and working habits on the island. He acquires the Indian takeaway habit.
In addition there are some tips on the world of work, just to give us an idea of what it's all about.

(S) THE STORYBOARD

Life for Ernst had certainly taken a turn for the better. By pure good luck he and Jenny had got a cottage in Hampstead less than a mile from his workplace. Jenny's hospital, too, was only a ten-minute drive away. Everything was coming up roses. Ernst was beginning to feel at home. But what about the working environment in England? On his first day at Cemokees, the English subsidiary, Ernst began to find things not the easiest[1]. Our hero was used to start[2] work at seven o'clock. So wanting to make a good impression he arrived at two minutes to seven. The security guard was not amused.

"Come on, mate, you don't expect me to believe that you want to start work at seven in the morning. I'm the only one here at this unearthly time and I wouldn't come if they didn't force me."

"No, no, we're talking past each other[3]. You see I'm nail new[4]. It's my first day."

The security guard was having none of it. "That's as may be, but you have to come here in normal working hours. Listen mate, I don't know you from Adam."

Poor old Ernst. "That's totally right. I'm not from here[5]."

"Yes, I can hear that. I'm sorry. Come back in two hours."

And come back he did. The morning's work was stressful, too. His colleagues used a lot of words our Ernst simply didn't know. People were friendly enough, though. It was soon lunchtime. "Come on Ernst," said Ronny. "Let's go for a pint at the Hampstead Heath." In the pub they drank a couple. Ronny was a humorous, open sort of fellow. It was time to pay for the snacks and beer and go back to the lion's den. Poor old Ernst. How painful[6]! "Ronny, could you lend me three pounds. I've forgotten my money."

Several hours later Ernst was at home eating an Indian takeaway. Jenny joined him an hour later and she was tired, too. Ernst felt sorry for him-

---

1 not as easy as he thought 2 was used to starting 3 talking at cross-purposes
4 I'm brand new 5 That's really true. I'm not from these parts. 6 how embarrassing!

self. "Oh, Jenny, the time went so slowly and such a bad weather[7] all afternoon. I could hardly stay awake." Ernst listed up the difficulties of the day. They gave him too much filing, too much invoice checking, the boss didn't have time to see him, etc., etc. "By the way, what sort of day did you have?"

"Oh, nothing much, one patient died on the operating table, we turned away a young boy with meningitis, there was a fight on the ward. It's all in a day's work."

Ernst felt small. "Shall I cook something for you. You look hungry. And you are as thin as beanstalk[8]."

"Oh, that'd be great and then I can jump into our old bath tub." Smiling Ernst, "Good idea, I'm sure you need it!"

LAUGHING at GRAMMAR

Question tag time. Fill in the gaps !

a) Boss: You should have been back from lunch at two o'clock, ________ ________?
Junior: I've been having my hair cut, ________ ________?
Boss: You did it in the firm's time, ________ ________?
Junior: Well, it grows in the firm's time, ________ ________?
Boss: Yes, but it doesn't all grow in the firm's time ________ ________?
Junior: Well, I didn't have all of it cut off!

b) When he was a student Ernst was short of money so he had to take a job in the local factory, as it paid good money. "Now," said the boss, "this is your first job, ________ ________? So you should sweep the floor." "But I'm studying at university," said Ernst. "Oh, you have a degree ________ ________?" said the boss. "In that case I'd better show you how to hold the brush, ________ ________?"

---

7 such bad weather 8 you're as thin as a rake

c) You can't help admiring our boss, _______ _______? If you don't, you don't work here any more.

d) Director of the company: You phoned my wife as I asked you to, _______ _______?

Secretary: Certainly, sir. I told her you would be late home from the office due to an unexpected conference.

Director: And she didn't ask anything else, _______ _______?

Secretary: Well, she asked if she could rely on that.

C CROSSING CULTURES

The world of work

Perhaps it might be the case in Germany that people flock to work at six-thirty or seven in the morning, take a twenty-minute lunch break and try to leave as early as they possibly can aided by flexi-time. This is not the case in "little England". Here normal people drift into work at eight-thirty or nine and stay loyally there until five. Often they go to the pub for an hour and this will include a couple of pints.

This coming together in the pub is an important part of the process of getting to know each other. When you are at the office in England for the first time, especially as a foreigner, it may seem that colleagues are aloof, somewhat stand-offish. The question is how to break through this barrier. There are several ways! For example, you could ask a colleague for advice. Little Englanders like that (so do Teutons, by the way). You might ask, "Where's the best place to eat?" or "I'm interested in doing some sport. Have you any idea where I could go?" The key point is not to isolate oneself. You have to make the others feel you want to be a member of the team.

A little hint. As mentioned above a lot of socializing is done in the pub. This can be a "let's pop into the local for a pint on the way home." Even if this is not your personal habit, it can be a vital stepping stone to becoming accepted. In such places ideas are exchanged about work (talking shop) and small-talking and networking is all around. I would even say these things are more significant than the communication inside the company. So remember, it might be a good idea to have "one for the road" with fellow-workers.

A few words on etiquette. If everybody arrives at the office dressed casually, do the same. If they all wear ties, you should wear one too. There are unofficial rules. It's not wise to buck the system. On the other hand you shouldn't be a creep either. It's all a slippery path, isn't it?

Be warned! Don't get into office politics! It will end badly. Keep your eyes and ears open. If everybody addresses the boss by his first name, you should do it, too. This is unlike the German situation. Using a first name does not imply any special closeness. It might be equivalent to "Sie, Michael" or "Sie, Helmuth"!

British business culture

Our companies in England are still organised traditionally, i.e., like a pyramid – a chain of command from the chairman and managing director in the clouds down to humblest slave in the cellar.

Somehow, there is an amateur approach to business in general. Englishmen seem to prefer to rely on their instincts rather than having well-worked out strategies and training. I believe this puts them at a disadvantage in international competition. They place great importance on simply "muddling through".

LAUGHING A LITTLE

Personnel manager: How well can you type?
Young secretary: My typing isn't very good, but I can delete at sixty-five words per minute!

Self-employed:
Now I work for myself I find the greatest difficulty is when I phone to say I'm sick.
I don't know whether or not to believe myself.

By working faithfully eight hours a day, you may eventually get to be a boss and work twelve hours a day.

"Now," said the interviewer, "before we start the interview, I'd like to ask you to take an intelligence test."
"An intelligence test?" queried the job applicant.
"The ad in the paper didn't mention intelligence. It stated you were looking for a research assistant for a Member of Parliament."

Officer junior. Please sir, can I have a day off next month?
Boss: What on earth for?
Junior: I'm getting married.
Boss: But you don't earn very much; you look like a tramp; you've no hope of being more than an office junior. What sort of idiot would marry you?
Junior: Your daughter, sir.

Angry boss: Alex, why are you late again this morning?
Alex: I overslept.
Angry boss: You mean you sleep at home as well?

PERFECT your PHRASALS

You know what's coming now ...
➜ Life had taken a turn for the better.

TAKE

take after	schlagen nach
take over	übernehmen
take to	Sympathie empfinden für
take with a pinch of salt	etwas mit Vorbehalt zur Kenntnis nehmen
take to drink	zu trinken beginnen
take the words out of somebody's mouth	jemandem das Wort aus dem Mund nehmen
take somebody wrong	jemanden missverstehen

LAUGHING A LITTLE

Can't see the wood for the trees!

Ernst: You know, Jenny, I think you should be more careful with your alcohol.

Jenny: Well, I'll take that comment with a pinch of salt. Anybody would think I had taken to drink to hear you talk.

Ernst: Well, actually you took the words right out of my mouth. I do think you're drinking too much. Don't take me wrong! I'm not trying to put you under pressure.

Jenny: I think you're sticking your nose in where it doesn't belong. How dare you presume to give me advice about things like that?

Ernst: Calm down!

Jenny: How can I calm down when you make comments like that? I'm so annoyed. I really need a drink.

CULTURAL QUIZ for BRAINWARES

1. Who works the most (hours per week)? Match the information! Germany, England, Italy
   a) 42.0 b) 42.4 c) 44.9
2. If an English person says he wants to "spend a penny, wash his hands or answer the call" what does he or she want?
3. The English do not die. They simply ________ on, ______ over, shuffle off or merely ________.
4. If an Englishman answers "mustn't grumble" (darf nicht jammern), what was the question?
5. Can you give definitions or descriptions of the following typical English institutions?
   a) Burberry b) Tartan c) pinstripe
   d) Punch e) Earl Grey

PLAYING with WORDS

Ernst is having a staff dialogue with his boss at the company in London. Help Ernst. Sometimes he can't find the phrases, sometimes he makes mistakes.

Boss: And you've been here for almost six months now. What are your feelings about things?

Ernst: Yes, at the beginning it wasn't the easiest. I had to _______ ________ a lot of extra responsibility. But I've got it together now.

Boss: I heard some members of staff were painting all sorts of black pictures for you.

Ernst: That's right. But as you told me at the beginning I have to ____________________ (es mit Vorbehalt zur Kenntnis nehmen) or I would __________________ (beginnen zu trinken). That's not happened. How ______________ (peinlich) that would have been.

Boss: I hope not. Well, I see you're settling in better now.

Ernst: Without any doubt! And now I've even got used to work these unusual hours, I mean nine to five with the occasional Saturday.

Boss: Good, because if you get promoted, the hours will become even more unusual, as you put it.

TIP of the day

If you want a job in Britain, prepare a short CV or résumé. You quote the names and addresses of two referees. Check the local newspaper, but also contact the local Chamber of Commerce. You can write directly to companies.

9

Ernst experiences his first encounters with hypermarkets and goes for a ten-kilometre walk through the shelves. He knows what it means to get worn out.
In addition you get some information on shops and buying in little old England. The island is a place where you need to know where you should shop.

S THE STORYBOARD

It was Saturday evening. Our two heroes had both had a long day at work. It was seven p.m. Ernst was feeling out of sorts. "Jenny, is this the way to spend a Saturday evening? We're both at work since nine o'clock this morning[1]. We've not bought any food. So we have to go into a restaurant[2] and that costs a lot of money."

Jenny was tired, too. She had to pull herself together. "Ernst, we've discussed it before. Food shops are still open. They're open till nine o'clock."
"Right, I always forget. It's longer as[3] in Germany. Shall we go and really make an evening of it?"

One hour later they were walking through the miles of shelves at the local Savewise, a well-known hypermarket chain. "I think we should sort out the food first. My goodness, look at all these steaks. There are hundreds of types. But why are they all packed[4]? Okay, let's have a roast beef, a swine cutlet and a fish[5]."

"Hey, slow down, we're only two people. When would we eat it all?"
"You're right. But I'm overrumbled[6] with all this choice."

Half an hour later.
Jenny, in a firm voice. "We certainly need some things for the cottage. Let's just check out the household sections. Here, look at these kitchen utensils. We can't manage without a set of meat knives, a Chinese wok, a fondue and a microwave."

"Great God, tear yourself together[7]! Meat knives, Jenny, you eat hardly meat[8]. And they cost £ 30. My God, I can buy the same knives for half the price in Germany."

"Well, we need some things. And by the way, what about a carpet? Look, there are cheap ones over there in the carpet department."

This sort of situation went on for the next two hours. On the way they passed through food, household articles, ladies clothes, cosmetics and

1 we've both been at work since nine
2 we have to eat at a restaurant
3 longer than, open later than
4 are they all in plastic packaging
5 some beef, a pork cutlet and some fish
6 I'm overwhelmed
7 pull yourself together, pull your socks up
8 you hardly eat meat

even "everything for the garden." "After all," stated Jenny, "we've got a very interesting old English garden at the back of the cottage."

Ernst, pushing a large supermarket trolley, was extremely nervous. "I know you think I'm being too sensible[9], but we've got a budget to keep." Jenny turned towards him with tears in her eyes. Ernst was beaten. "I know, I know, you live only one time[10]."

LAUGHING at GRAMMAR

Ernst has that illness called P.P.P. from time to time –
Pesky preposition problems. We'll give him a few workshops.
Can you help?

a) A bargain is something you cannot use _________ a price you cannot resist.

b) I found a real bargain in the supermarket. The normal 50 pence tin of baked beans was reduced ________ 75 p ________ 65p!

c) Lady customer: May I try _____ that dress _____ the window?
Assistant: Well, we'd prefer it if you used the changing room.

d) The newly opened shopping centre has three tailors – right _____ _______ each other. By the way all three tailors are called Jacob Silverstein. The first has a sign ____ his shop which proclaims: "Jacob Silverstein – High Class Tailor". The second tailor has a sign ______ "Silverstein – The Tailor of Distinction". The third tailor has a smaller notice _______ his shop. _______ it was written "Silverstein's Tailors – Main Entrance".

9 sensitive 10 you only live once

C CROSSING CULTURES

Shopping in the new millennium

Of course in the old days (exactly what are they, these old days), people went to the many small shops for most of their needs. Well, these tiny stand-alone shops have mostly disappeared under the attack of the super-market and hypermarket chains. But it is still possible to find a corner shop selling bits and pieces. Most of these are, in fact, mini-supermarkets run by industrious Asians from Pakistan or India. These were once the old off-licences, shops for selling spirits and beers to be consumed "off" the premises, hence "off-licences". By the way, nowadays they are often called "Patelleries" after the common Asian surname Patel.

Today you can get anything in supermarket chains. The most famous are Sainsbury, Marks & Spencer, Safeway and Tesco. Here you buy Indian, Chinese, Italian, Spanish, Japanese as well your typical English steaks & hamburgers. As far as I'm concerned my major dislike is the kilometres of walking around the shelves and the huge choice. It makes me tired and nervous. Others like it though. You can see little Englanders on Saturday and Sunday carting great carloads of booty away from the hypermarkets. Where do they get their money from?

Window-shopping. Not only for poor people, this is the art of monitor-ing exactly what's on offer in window displays. It's especially useful to knock down a bargain here or there. You can also come back later to grab your booty.

There are chains of supermarkets offering everything. One type is the chain-store offering newspapers and magazines. There are thousands of different magazines in Britain. Titles include Woman, Woman's Own, House & Garden, Vogue, everything from Jane to Zena. They cover topics such as Homeopathy, DIY and computers, journals for the handicapped, minority groups, the young and the not-so-young. And all yours for less than £ 2, my boy. What more do you want? The chains which stock these include John Menzies & WH Smith. If you want to know about sizes and costs of things in England, please refer to Ernst's first trip to England in "Better your English".

LAUGHING A LITTLE

Sales assistant: Madam, this cooker is very economical.
It'll pay for itself in no time at all.
Shopper: Well, as soon as it does, send it over to my place!

Life was simpler before credit cards. You didn't have to wait till the end of the month to find out how poor you were.

I was going to buy a copy of the Power of Positive Thinking, but then I thought "What the hell good would that do?"
Ronald Shakes

If it weren't for bad luck I wouldn't have any luck at all.

As I hurtled through space, one thought kept crossing my mind. Every part of this capsule was supplied by the lowest bidder.
John Glynn

I once read an advertisement in a woman's magazine that went something like this:
Do you want him to remember you and think of you when you're not there? Always wear the same perfume when you go out with him. The sense of smell is one of the greatest memory prodders. He'll learn to associate that scent with you and think of you every time he smells it, even on someone else.
My God, does the woman think I'm a Labrador Retriever (a dog)?
Gilbert Harding

PERFECT your PHRASALS

Ernst is in trouble.

➜ Ernst was feeling out of sorts.

FEEL (2)

feel bad	sich schlecht fühlen
feel at ease	sich wohl fühlen
feel something in one's bones	etwas instinktiv spüren
feel like (doing something)	Lust haben, etwas zu tun
feel out of place	sich fehl am Platze fühlen

LAUGHING A LITTLE

Consequences

Mike: I reckon we did wrong when we stole that radio from the supermarket. I felt at ease when I was doing it, but now I feel bad.

Terry: Don't start talking like that. It was your idea anyway. It's all your fault. I think somebody saw us. I feel it in my bones that something's going to happen.
(Doorbell rings)

Mike: Who is it?

Voice: It's the police, sir, I'd like to talk to Mr Michael Laver, please.

9 CULTURAL QUIZ for BRAINWARES

1. If you are eating Tandori what sort of ethnic restaurant are you in?
   a) Chinese   b) Indian   c) Singapore
2. What would you use the following for?
   a) a trolley: b) a carpet: c) a changing room:
3. Which is the larger shopping outlet: a supermarket or a hypermarket?
4. How could you translate the German phrase "Tante-Emma-Laden?
5. Is the population of England
   a) 48 million   b) 55 million   c) 65 million?
6. The Royal Family in England, you know, the Queen & Co. Are they
   a) German   b) Greek   c) Anglo-Saxon
   in descent (in their origins)?
7. How do the English refer to the rest of Europe?
   a) firm land   b) the mainland   c) the continent
8. When an English person calls you a good sport, what does he really mean?
   a) you're a good loser
   b) you're good at your event (football, athletics, etc.)
   c) you're okay, you're a fair bloke, thumbs up!
9. What was originally sold in off-licences in England?
10. If you want to buy five or ten steaks where would you rather be?
   a) Smiths   b) Tesco   c) Aldi

PLAYING with WORDS

Ernst is at a supermarket. He's getting into trouble with one of the assistants. Can you help him? Some of his phrases are wrong, some he can't remember.

Ernst: I'm looking for somebody to help me for five minutes. It's terrible.

Assistant: Sorry, sir. We're very busy. How can I help you?

Ernst: Well look, all these lamb chops are packed. I'd like to have them separately.

Assistant: Sorry, sir. They are all in vacuum packaging and individually selected.

Ernst: Well, I (Lust haben) going somewhere else. It's all so mechanised, so unpersonal. I really don't (sich wohl fühlen) without the personal touch.

Assistant: I suggest you go elsewhere then, sir.

TIP of the day

Drive to your local Tesco hypermarket or their competitors for stocking up for the week. They all have special discount systems. For emergencies in the evening go to the off-licence. Go to the markets for fresh veg and fruit. It's dirt cheap.

10

Ernst gets involved in that good old traditional British pastime, the party. There he gets to know how some Brits can very easily misbehave when the alcohol is flowing.
There are many words and phrases for relaxing and partying. Think of "chilling out", "letting your hair down" and "letting it all hang out".
You also get some tips on partying, the consequences and the remedies or cures.

S THE STORYBOARD

The weeks went by. Life was beginning to settle down. Ernst was taking the bull by the horns and trying to integrate himself to the utmost. Sometimes Ernst would go out to meet other people. "I don't want to get bored with Jenny by being with her too often, so to say[1]," Ernst explained to himself.

And so it was that our hero was invited to a party by Viv, a girl from his office. "Come on, Ernst, let your hair down. Chill out a bit. We'll drink a few lagers and talk about the birds and the bees." Ernst was mystified. "I'm not keen to[2] speak about the animal world, football is more my case[3]."

That evening (clinking of glasses, loud voices) Viv had spent most of the time keeping within arm's length of Ernst. She waved at a tall blond girl, a friend of hers, to come over and meet her latest victim. "Hi, Jill, come and introduce yourself to our German bloke from work."

"Hi, I'm Jill. What's your handle?" Ernst had lost the thread again. What had this to do with doors? "Sorry?" "I mean what do you call yourself? Tom, Dick or Harry?" "Oh, I see. Ernst. My name's Ernst." Ernst felt a bit stupid.

"What's a lovely foreigner like you doing in this boring place?" "He's enjoying himself with an interesting local girl like me." Jill showed her teeth in half a smile. "Oh, are you his keeper for tonight, then?"

Ernst decided it was time to say something. "Yes, I'm working in the same company like[4] Viv. I'm engineer[5]." Jill seemed to be impressed. "You mean you've done a degree? Wow!" This was getting a bit embarrassing. "Well, I made my study in machine building[6]."

Jill was getting a bit drunk. "Come on, Ernst, let me get you a drink. You look too serious." She slipped her arm into his. "Hey, that's a bit too much." Viv had also had a drop too much. Another loud voice boomed from behind Ernst. "What are you doing with my girlfriend?" Ernst

1 so to speak, as it were
2 I'm not keen on speaking
3 my cup of tea, my thing
4 same company as
5 I'm an engineer
6 I studied mechanical engineering

looked around. "And that still[7]," he said to himself as he stared into the half drunken eyes of a giant of a man, a mixture of an Australian rugby player and an Austrian weight-lifter. "I'm sure you have it in the wrong throat." The brain-dead athlete was not impressed. He pushed Ernst aggressively. "You'll be getting it in the wrong throat if you're not careful."

Viv intervened. She stood in between the two men. "The pair of you should pull yourselves together. You, Ernst, you're in a foreign country. You should know better. You, Peter, I wouldn't even expect you to know better. You can't make a silk purse out of a sow's ear." The two men crept away. Ernst felt badly misunderstood.

LAUGHING at GRAMMAR

Pretty Prepositions – Workshop II

a) "I have been asked to get married hundreds _____ times," said Jill proudly. "_____ whom?" asked Viv. "My mum and dad," replied Jill.

b) An Englishman boarded a train _____ a shaggy dog and sat _____ an Irishman. Paddy looked _____ the dog for a while and then said, "And what type _____ dog might that be?" The surly Englishman replied, "It's a cross _____ an ape and an Irishman." Paddy was quick _____ his reply. "You mean it's related _____ both of us."

c) Two husbands were leaning ❒ at / ❒ on the bar:
Did you give your wife a lecture ❒ in / ❒ on economy like I told you to?
"Yes, I certainly did." "And what was the result?" "I've got to give ❒ up / ❒ off smoking."

d) The wife was nervous as she got _____ the wheel of their new car _____ the first time. "I hardly know what to do," she said. "Just imagine I'm driving," he replied.

---

7 that's all I need

C CROSSING CULTURES

All about parties

The British like their parties and use any excuse to have them. They are often spontaneous events except, of course, for the time and day. In English we talk about "throwing a party" which might give a clue about it. Really, if you think about it, some parties are actually an extension of the drink after work phenomenon, but taking place at someone's "pad", a colloquial and chilled out label for a flat or house.

These sort of parties, which can be organised through work or just amongst friends have one thing in common – lakes of alcohol. The British have always been good at drinking other nationalities' national drinks. In addition to their own varieties of beer including real ales, lagers, milds and bitters and whisky (Scottish, of course, not English, although the English have stolen that drink from the Scots too), little Englanders have succeeded in importing and imbibing huge quantities of port from Portugal, sherry from Spain, and it goes without saying wine from everywhere it grows. Add to this plenty of Vodka (it doesn't smell like some other drinks do) and you've got a party.

We've all seen what can happen at these parties and poor old Ernst experienced it at first hand too. When people drink too much they can become pushy or even primitive and aggressive. It's all not helped by the unwritten rule that you have to "bring a bottle" when you go to the party. What does all this mean? Well, inevitably it will lead to another British symptom, the hangover or the upset stomach on the following day. This upset stomach is usually regarded as a problem of the bowels. This bowel question is almost a complex amongst the islanders. We learn to fear it in our childhoods. Bowel movements must be very regular! A visit to the smallest room is the only correct way to start the day. If this doesn't happen the Brit talks about "getting out of bed on the wrong side" or "starting on the wrong foot".

Just look in the shops. There are a hundred thousand cures and medicines for all this. Famous old names such as Andrews Liver Salt, Enos, Milk of Magnesia or Cod Liver Oil. The worse they smell or taste, the better for you.

LAUGHING A LITTLE

The art of medicine consists of amusing the patient
while Nature cures the disease.

Voltaire

Worried patient: Doctor, I'm very worried. I'm still suffering from exhaustion and fatigue when I come home from work every evening.

Doctor: Oh, that's nothing to worry about. Just have a few drinks before dinner, that'll soon wake you up.

Patient: Thanks, but when I consulted you before you told me to cut out drinking completely.

Doctor: Yes, so I did. But that was last week, old chap, and medical science has progressed enormously since then.

I have finally come to the conclusion that a good reliable set of bowels
is worth more to a man than any quantity of brains.

Josh Billings

PERFECT your PHRASALS

Here is some more medicine to cure Ernst's problem.

TAKE

take someone down a peg or two	in die Schranken weisen
take the chair	den Vorsitz übernehmen
take on	annehmen
take in	verarbeiten, verstehen
take over	übernehmen
take to	Gefallen finden an
take up	anfangen, ausüben

LAUGHING A LITTLE

Industrial Democracy!

Boss:	I've called you all together to tell you that we have decided to take on a lot of extra work in the next month.
Union representative:	What does this mean for my members? Will we have to work overtime? What's in it for us? We need time to take all these facts in.
Boss:	Since you're asking, I'll tell you what has happened. We have taken over a small company. It means we have to do the work of that company as well as our own. That will mean overtime and extra money for you, the employees. I'm sure you'll take to that idea.
Union representative:	I don't know if my members are willing to take up your interesting offer. It's their free time, you know.
Boss:	Mister, I'm not offering! I'm telling you!

CULTURAL QUIZ for BRAINWARES

1. Explain "what's your handle?"
a) your point of view **b)** your Christian name **c)** your job

2. What's meant by "let's take the bull by the horns"?
a) Let's kill this problem
b) Let's discuss the problem
c) Let's tackle the problem in a determined way

3. You try to pay for your meal with a credit card. It doesn't work. "Und das noch." How would you say it?
a) and still that **b)** that's all I need **c)** and that comes too

4. You can't make a silk purse out of a sow's ear. What is the German proverb?

5. What about some opposites for the linguistic brainwares? These opposites appeared somewhere in this chapter.
   a) confident b) uncertain
   c) jump off / disembark d) fail

6. Guess what "gate-crashing" a party is?
   a) destroying furniture when drunk
   b) coming into the party uninvited

7. We're talking about a famous English short drink made from juniper (Wacholderbeerbaum). What is it?

8. Fish & chips used to be eaten in a special way
   a) with a wooden fork
   b) out of a newspaper
   c) in a round bowl

9. Probably the most eaten food (I use the word loosely) in a pub with your beer or drink is:
   a) cheese sandwich b) egg & bacon c) crisps

10. Henry VIII had six wives but what did he die of?
    a) a nervous disease
    b) a sexual disease
    c) overeating and drinking

PLAYING with WORDS

Help our Ernst. He's forgotten some words and has got others wrong!

1. I had much to drink at the party last night and this morning I had some pressure in my head, so to speak.
2. Ernst: Well, I can tell you honestly, these parties are not (mein Fall).
3. Boss: I heard you were out drinking pretty hard with some members of staff last night.

   Ernst: No, not really, well yes. Actually you've (in den falschen Hals gekriegt).
4. Ernst: You really don't like Viv very much, or?
   Jill: Well, since you mention it, no!
   Ernst: I know. She needs (in die Schranken weisen).
5. Ernst: Where've you been? I was awaiting you at 7 p.m.
   Jenny: Well, to tell the truth, England is getting so violent.
   Ernst: I know, and you're thinking of (ausüben) Karate or self-defence.
   Jenny: You've hit the nail on the head!

TIP of the day

When you go to a party, take a bottle of wine, don't get more than merry, don't take any drugs and remember, you never know who'll be there. You've got a life after the party.

11

Working hard is all well and good but you can't do it indefinitely or you'll get ill. In this chapter we find Ernst checking out what sort of entertainment is available. London has a lot of it, so he's spoilt for choice.
There is also a comment on the various areas of what we describe as culture.

S THE STORYBOARD

Both Ernst and Jenny found themselves having to work a lot of hours. Ernst complained that he hasn't expected to do so much overtime and at least it was paid back in Germany. Jenny, who was tired of his moaning and felt that she had the harder job with all her patients, told him in no uncertain words: "You wanted to come here. It was your free choice."

Ernst felt misunderstood, but he realised that he should take more care of Jenny. "I should rather[1] do something in private with Jennybell." His mind was racing. "I could spend her a meal[2] this evening, but that's not special enough."

"Jenny, where's that brochure with the entertainment in London in it?"

"You mean the What's On? – It's on top of the telly."

"Right," thought our charmer, "we have to undertake some steps[3]." Ernst leafed through the journal. He saw advertisements for meeting places, groups with special interests, the theatre, films (hundreds of them), clubs of every sort. "This looks good." He thought of suggesting some sport. A weight-training centre or fitness club.

"We can get us fit[4]. But then she might complain she does enough physical stuff at her job." His eye travelled further. Musicals. "Well, what about that?" "Jenny, I've got an idea. Why don't we go to Evita? The most people[5] say it's wonderful. It could be a relaxing weekend." "Oh, Ernst that's a marvellous idea. We could have an exotic meal afterwards and a bottle of excellent wine accompanied by glasses of warm saki. What a change from all this work!"

"Hey slowly, we mustn't drink too much alcohol. You can get a headache. I only drink when I want to let the pig out[6]." Jenny was still in a good mood. "There's really a lot of choice of what to do in your leisure time here in London, isn't there?"

---

1 I ought to
2 I could invite her to dinner
3 take some steps, make a move
4 do some sport; get fit
5 most people
6 let my hair down

"There certainly is," commented Ernst. "But I think the most interesting things are the theatres, operas and cinemas. Look how many new films are running at the cinemas[7]. You could go to a different one every day."

So our young lovers went off to the musical. They enjoyed it and Jenny even shed a tear. Afterwards at the Japanese restaurant Ernst shed a couple of tears, too. One when he ate sushami and dipped his raw tuna fish into a very sharp horseradish sauce. The other when he got the bill for the meal.

LAUGHING at GRAMMAR

Let's check out verb tenses!

a) A theatrical agent is someone who __________ (believe) that an actor takes 90 per cent of his money.

b) I've got a very ambitious agent – he __________ (always open) offices overseas. At the moment I __________ (be) out of work in seventeen countries.

c) Director: Well, I __________(look) at your screen test and, quite frankly, it would take an act of Congress to get you into the movies.

d) A famous actor bumped into a friend at a Hollywood party and started to tell him about the success of his latest film. "They __________ (love) it," he said, "and they __________ (love) me in it too! The audience reaction __________ (be) fantastic and you should read the reviews – they __________ (call) me the new Laurence Olivier! We __________ (talk) about Oscar nominations here! And they've got me on the front of Time next week! Anyway Jim, here I am going on about myself and I haven't even asked about you. Tell me, what you __________ (think) of me in the film?"

6 let my hair down 7 films are being shown

e) An editor is one who _________ (separate) the wheat from the chaff and _________ (print) the chaff. *Adlai Stevenson*

f) Most of the time Marlon Brando _________ (sound) as if he _________ (have) a mouth full of wet toilet paper.

C CROSSING CULTURES

Modern culture in England

To reduce culture to terms that all of us can deal with on one DIN A4 page or less we should forget Shakespeare, Byron, Goethe and all the rest and concentrate on what's really going on. Going on is some theatre, a lot of films from home and abroad, the hundred thousand forms of "in" music and perhaps some bits of informative radio.

The radio

Many people thought that this medium would be overshadowed by television and eventually more or less disappear except for a few specialist broadcasts. This did not happen. Radio is very much alive in Britain. There are more than twenty stations to tune into. We have BBC Radio 4 which offers only talk shows, and independent stations which can be very high-brow or plain rude. Radio also provides an information service for the millions of commuters, a weather service and traffic information etc. It provides a great variety of entertainment.

Television

This is dealt with in another chapter of which it forms the basis.

The stage

The capital city, London, is certainly the focus of drama and theatrical activity in Britain. Even so the smaller towns also have their own offerings performed in many cases by amateurs doing it for the love of the sport, as it were.
Back in London the plays and musicals have their homes in the West End of London. Often you have to book months in advance if you want

to be sure of a seat. For a hit show you can expect to pay up to £40.
A few hints when going to a show. First, don't be late! It's bad manners and they won't let you in anyway. You may get in at the next interval. Please note, there is no smoking at these performances. In some theatres you are not allowed to take photographs or even have the equipment with you.

The concert

Concerts on a small scale are given by buskers in many of London's public places. Sometimes these performances are very professional. Many of these street players are hoping for the big break.
Concerts at Wembley in London are given by top names such as Michael Jackson, Oasis or Sting. In terms of classical music the most popular event is probably the Proms, especially the Last Night at the Proms where millions of little Englanders wave their Union Jacks (remember what it is?) when they hear Rule Britannia (a sort of unofficial national anthem).

LAUGHING A LITTLE

Ernst: I took my girlfriend to the theatre last night, but we only saw the first Act and then we had to leave.
John: Why was that?
Ernst: Well, on the programme it said: "Act Two: Two days later" – and we couldn't stay in the theatre that long.

The theatre-goer was getting increasingly annoyed at the two women in the row in front who were talking to each other throughout the play. Finally, he leaned forward and said to one of the women, "Excuse me, but I can't hear a word." "I should hope not," said the woman. "This is a private conversation."

I'm not saying he's ugly but he's got a perfect face for radio.

Radio is a device that allows people who have nothing to say to talk to people who aren't listening.

PERFECT your PHRASALS

You know what's coming. Some more phrasals for Ernst and you perhaps.

➜ He wasn't expected to do so much overtime.

DO

do one's best	sein Möglichstes tun
do one's bit	seinen Teil beisteuern
do it up	renovieren
do with	(gut) brauchen (können)
done for	ruiniert sein
do away with	abschaffen, niederreißen

LAUGHING A LITTLE

A challenge with a difference

Jenny: Shall we buy this house? It's a bit old, but we can do it up.

Ernst: Jenny, if we bought this place we could do with a team of workmen. It's a ruin.

Jenny: Rubbish! W could move straight in. I know it's a bit shabby, but it'll be all right.

Ernst: Are you blind? The house is more or less done for. Look at the roof! We'll have to do away with the roof for a start.

Jenny: That's it! That's what we need. A real challenge!

11

CULTURAL QUIZ for BRAINWARES

1. How many main TV channels are there in Britain?

2. Which of the following authors is really best known to the English?
   a) Charles Dickens b) Beatrix Potter c) Shakespeare

3. What's the name given to the underground that runs through London?

4. What's the odd man out in these newspapers?
   a) Guardian b) Mirror
   c) Sun d) People

5. It's a difficult question but can you name Britain's most famous distance-learning university (Fernstudium)?

6. In which part of London do most of the musicals and shows take place?
   a) East End b) West End c) City of London

7. What's the name of that famous book with the Hobbit creature, dragons and wars on a fantasy Earth in pre-history?
   The L_______ of the R_______.

8. Which is the most successful British football club of all time?

9. What do you call people who don't eat meat or fish?

10. Roald Atkinson is the actor. Who is his most famous character?

PLAYING with WORDS

1. Ernst is going to a party on Friday evening. He wants to
   a) let the pig out
   b) let his hair down
   c) let it loose.

2. At work Ernst (tut sein Möglichstes) to organise his tasks efficiently.

3. Jenny is tired of the work at the hospital. She intends to (abschaffen) the weekend work.

4. Ernst had the idea of buying an old cottage and (renovieren) it.

5. **a)** People who travel to work every day by train = c____________
   b) A play where songs are sung too = m____________
   c) People who watch or listen to a performance = a____________

TIP of the day

Try to adapt to the situation.
When at work, fit in. Don't be a square peg in a round hole.
At the theatre or musical, be punctual. Think of the others.

12

In this episode we find our hero in difficulty. He injures himself on foreign soil. Now he's dependent on specialists "nit von doo!". Ernst is off to a hospital in the National Health System. He must "through"[1] as they say.
We also get some information on what's happening in medicine, teeth etc. Good luck, Ernst!

1 he has to manage it

S THE STORYBOARD

As we all know Ernst thought himself to be something of an athlete, and especially a footballer. As Jenny always told him, "you can't be that fit. You smoke like a chimney." Our Ernst felt that he had to prove himself. So one Saturday morning he went down on to Hampstead Heath and joined in a game of football. It was raining and dangerous. "I have to be careful or I'll do myself a lot of damages[2]." But, of course, it happened anyway. Although he scored two goals and Jenny was impressed, he also managed to tear his cartilage. Poor old Ernst was in a lot of pain when he was delivered, in the company of his nervous princess, Jenny, to the Hampstead Sports Clinic.

"Thank God it's located in the near[3]," sighed our wounded hero. The desk nurse asked him what the problem was. "I don't know exactly. Eventually[4] I twisted my knee or something like that. It pains[5]. The nurse did not seem particularly sympathetic. "Okay, go through to the waiting room and wait till you're called. First room on the left."

"Come on," whispered Jenny. "Owww! I can't walk so fast. With other words[6] I'm half-crippled." "Oh, don't make so much fuss. You'll be okay." The doctor called Ernst in. "Doctor, I'm privately insured. I ..."

"Mr. Lachnit, private insurance or not isn't of any importance here. Just tell me what happened."

"Oh, right. Well, I was playing football and I kicked the ball very hard, by the way I scored two goals ..."

"Well, you should have thought more carefully about it before you injured yourself." Ernst felt a bit stupid.

"I tried too hard. I just didn't want to blame myself[7]." The doctor wasn't interested. "Could you come through into the radiology? We'll just do a tomograph of your left knee."

An hour later Ernst and Jenny were called in for a consultation with the doctor. "I'm afraid your cartilage is torn. You'll have to come in for a small operation."

---

2 damage
3 in the vicinity, nearby
4 perhaps
5 it hurts
6 in other words
7 to make a fool of myself

12 "Oh no!" Ernst was really upset. "How long will I have to stay in? How long will I be off work? Will I be able to walk normally again?"

The doctor was severe. "It's no good crying over spilt milk." "You're right!" Ernst pulled himself together. "These little things don't disturb my great spirit[8]."

LAUGHING at GRAMMAR

Pesky prepositions – Workshop III

a) Visitor: Excuse me, but could you tell me which ward Olga Hennit is ______?
Receptionist: Ah yes. Wasn't she the lady who was run _____ _____ a steamroller this morning?
Visitor: Yes.
Receptionist: Well, she's ______ wards 7, 8, 9 and 10.

b) Before they admitted me _____ this private hospital, the doctor interviewed me to find _______ what illness I could afford to have.

c) She's a lousy nurse. She couldn't even put a dressing ______ a salad.

d) Patient: _____ the operation, will I be able to play tennis?
Surgeon: Of course you will.
Patient: That's great, because I never could ________.

8 when the going gets tough, the tough get going

(C) CROSSING CULTURES

Medicine in the UK

It's bad enough to get ill anywhere. It's worse to become sick when you're away from home. We saw it with Ernst and his footballing nonsense. So what about medicine in Britain? Well, we have our National Health System. It's never been perfect and people criticize it as often as they can. However, in terms of the latest advances in medicine it often leads the world.

It's important, to begin with, who your doctor is, where you live and the nature of your illness. The first thing you have to do is move into your apartment, then you register with a doctor. Surgery hours are usually 10 a.m. to 12 noon and 5 p.m. to 7 p.m. Please make an appointment!

Between those times many doctors are doing their rounds at various hospitals. If you need to go into hospital, you'll have to get a referral from your doctor. Remember! In Britain hospitals are generally understaffed and bed space is problematical.

All treatment is free under National Health; you pay for the prescription if you're over 18. Under 16 all treatment and prescriptions are free. The clinic will give you the prescription, you have to go to the chemists to get it made up.

Most patients do a bit of self-medicating. They treat themselves for minor ailments. It's better than wasting the busy doctor's time. Of course, antibiotics are only available on prescription (who needs them, anyway?). The great problem with the system is if you need surgery. You may have to wait several months for it. Doctors in hospitals are totally overworked. So what about private medicine? Well, it's expensive. I myself have a private medical insurance, it costs me DM 210 per month. This might seem little for a German citizen, but for us it's a lot. In an English hospital you will not be pampered if you have special wishes, but you will get a proper medical treatment.

Dental treatment? It's about the same as the medical treatment but not so complicated since there are not so many patients. Students under eighteen get it free. Adults pay 75%, the remaining 25% comes under the NHS.

LAUGHING A LITTLE

The desire to take medicine is perhaps the greatest feature which distinguishes man from animals.

William Osler

I came in here in all good faith to help my country. I don't mind giving a reasonable amount [of blood], but a pint ... why that's nearly an armful. I'm sorry, I'm not walking around with an empty arm for anybody.

Ray Galton

I don't mind dying, the trouble is you feel so bloody stiff the next day.

PERFECT your PHRASALS

Poor old Ernst.

➜ It's no good crying over spilt milk.

CRY

cry one's head off	in Tränen zerfließen
cry on someone's shoulder	sich bei jemandem ausweinen
cry wolf	blinden Alarm schlagen

LAUGHING A LITTLE

Cry babies!

Susan: Oh, I'm so afraid I won't pass my exam. Then I'll have wasted so much time with all this preparation. Look at these practice questions. They're too difficult for me.

Kurt: You know your trouble is that you cry wolf at every small problem. Then you make yourself nervous and half-crazy till you cry your head off every time you think about it.

Susan: Oh, you've no feelings for other people's problems. I need a shoulder to cry on and not a lecture about psychology.

Kurt: That's it. You're just looking for sympathy instead of getting on and doing your work. It's typical of your generation.

CULTURAL QUIZ for BRAINWARES

1. What do the letters NHS stand for?

2. Can you guess how many people are privately insured in Britain?
a) 10 million **b)** 7 million **c)** 3 million

3. What is the document called written by a general practitioner with which you can go to a specialist at the hospital?

4. What's the English for the "Rezept" from a doctor?
a) prescription **b)** receipt **c)** recipe

5. Can you find two more words for sickness?

6. At the dentists. If you want a tooth "gezogen" what do you say?
a) pull it out **b)** draw it out **c)** remove it

7. You want the dentist to put a new top part on your tooth. What is it called?
a) a crown **b)** a top **c)** a cover

8. Away from all that medical stuff! What is Hadrian's Wall and why was it built?

9. If two people married in England, what about their rings?
a) fourth finger, right hand
b) fourth finger, left hand
c) no ring

10. Fairy tales. How do you begin them?
a) It was once a ...
b) Once upon a time there was ...
c) There was once a ...

12

PLAYING with WORDS

1. Can you support Ernst at the hospital and correct his mistakes?

Doctor: Now where exactly does it hurt, Mr Lachnit?
Ernst: Well, it pains me in the area of my stomach.
Doctor: Where about? Here?
Ernst: Ouch! Yes there! It's in the near of my ribs.
Doctor: When did the trouble start? When did you first notice it?
Ernst: Yesterday morning. After my jog. Doctor, doctor, I'm sure it's my liver. I'm going to die.
Doctor: Mr Lachnit, you're reacting too quickly.
Ernst: I'm sure I have some damages in my body. Liver, heart, gall bladder. Somehow every time I make sport here I blame myself. I get injured.

2. Find the correct term.

a) doctor's visits = ____________
b) heal yourself = ____________
c) pay money, cover your risks = ____________
d) spoil somebody, a child = ____________

TIP of the day

Don't think you become priority case because you've got private insurance. Not if your using NHS facilities. Watch out for snobism.

We all know that Ernst has been working very hard in London and needs a break. Off he goes with Jenny on a short motor car tour in the countryside. He tests the joys of bed & breakfast and enjoys some of Britain's greenery.
There's more information on camping, hotels and B & B and a wealth of tips.

13 (S) THE STORYBOARD

Ernst, of course, wanted to see as much of Britain as he could during his time on the island. One of his excursions took them to Cornwall. The county of Cornwall, together with Devon and Somerset make up the West Country. It was originally a Celtic area though nowadays the language is no longer spoken. They were driving down windy, narrow country roads. "Hey, drive more slowly. If anything comes the other way we're dead." "No fear[1]. I have a lot of experience on country streets[2]. Remember, I'm from Heidelberg. It's the same problem there, too." Before Jenny could bat an eyelid they shot round a corner and straight into the side of a tractor. Jenny's car was badly damaged along the right side. "You bloody fool," she screeched. Their conversation will be left out for the moment.

An hour later they pulled into a farmhouse having seen a B & B sign hanging outside. The bedroom was clean and rustic, with a wooden bed in the middle of the room. There was an open fireplace with a fire burning. That evening our two lovers consoled themselves in front of the fire with one or two pints of the local cider, called scrumpy. It's like very dry apple wine but much stronger. After two pints they were both drunk. "The room is turning[3]. I don't feel so good."

The following morning they found themselves in front of one of those famous English breakfasts. "In the moment[4] I really don't feel like eating all this," moaned Ernst. "Look, it's all lying in fat. All those baked beans, mushrooms, bacon and this piece of bread cooked in fat. The farmer's wife told me it's all to eat[5]."

"I'm sure she did. It's all fresh from the farmyard. No battery hens here." "That's true. But we don't know for how long. It's all a question of who can offer the products cheaper. There's so much concurrence[6] from the factory producers. I would think it's not rentable[7] for a farm like this to exist." Jenny agreed with him.

1 don't worry!
2 country roads
3 my head is spinning
4 at the moment / at the minute
5 it should be eaten up; it's all to be eaten up
6 competition
7 rentabel = viable, profitable; rentable = mietbar

After breakfast they both had to lie down for an hour. They both felt sick, whether it was from the English breakfast or the cider from the evening before. "No problem," grunted Ernst. "It belongs to[8] the culture of a country. Let's go for a country walk."

LAUGHING at GRAMMAR

Let's check out verb tenses!

a) When I told my cousin that I ________ (fix) him up with a date with an attractive librarian he asked: what part of Libraria does she come from?

b) We're continually hearing about the terrible crime rate in America, but is it true? For example, when I arrived in New York a few months ago, a man came up to me and asked if I __________ (want) to buy a watch. I asked him how much it __________ (cost). "Sssh!" said the man, "the guy next to you is still wearing it."

c) It was long ago in my life as a simple reporter that I decided that facts ________ (must) never get in the way of truth.

d) The sales manager had run out of ways to motivate his men. Finally, he called them together and said that the day before he __________ (launch) a sales contest. And that the man who __________ (win) ________ (get) to keep his job.

8 it's part of

C CROSSING CULTURES

Touring round Britain

Bed & Breakfast is an old English tradition which gives great help to visitors. It costs about £25 to £40 per night and gives people from towns a chance to integrate into the homes of country people. They are not like hotels, the service is informal, and normally warm and friendly. Rooms of this type are often quite basic and full of the personal objects of the family.

Most Brits are fascinated by the (in)famous breakfast the morning after. It consists of sausages, eggs, toasts, tea and jam baked beans. It can be very nice to be served a hot breakfast of sausages, eggs sunny side up, fragrant jam and at the same time gaze through the window into green fields and oak trees.

The more adventurous of us may have been on camping holidays in the south of France, Italy or Portugal. There you have facilities to cater for every wish – car wash, waste water disposal, camp-site restaurants. You can camp in Britain too. The word camping is the only similarity. Here you are down to the barest essentials, perhaps a toilet, maybe electricity if you are lucky. You have to be a hardy adventurer if you want to do this in Britain. You know, the sort of people who carry mountain tents on their backs and food tablets to last a week. The ones who can really read the military ordinance survey maps.

We have hotels in England and excellent ones. These are historical institutions, sometimes five hundred years old. There are new custom-built ones, too and they are often cheaper. But who wants to go there? The charm of the ancient places is something different. I remember going for a long weekend to Cornwall or Devon in the south west. A twelfth century hotel, downstairs the open fire was crackling away. A local dish of cottage pie and a pint or two of real ale and off to bed. The floorboards in the bedroom creaked with hundreds of years of history. It was great!

LAUGHING A LITTLE

I'd never stayed in a hotel where the service was so slow.
If you ordered anything from them,
you had to leave a forwarding address.

Landlady: Rooms overlooking the sea are £5 extra.
Guest: How much if I promise not to look?

My room was so small, I couldn't brush my teeth sideways.

What a classy hotel! The towels were so thick and fluffy
I hardly could close my suitcase.

Guest: I'd like to complain about the facilities in this hotel. They're practically non-existent.

Landlady: Well, well. Who got up on the wrong side of the floor today?

PERFECT your PHRASALS

It's a never ending story. Ernst's problems continue.

→ Their conversation will be left out.

LEAVE

leave alone	in Ruhe lassen
leave off	aufhören, aufgeben
leave over	übrig bleiben, übrig lassen
leave someone out in the cold	jemanden links liegen lassen
leave well alone	die Finger davonlassen
leave someone's stamp on	den Stempel aufdrücken

13

LAUGHING A LITTLE

The competitive world!

Steve: Hi, Seb, you're looking unhappy. What's happened?

Seb: I've been left out in the cold. They haven't chosen me for the Olympics.

Steve: Well, your performances haven't been as good as they used to be. But it should have been enough to get into the team.

Seb: It's all because of those discussions I had on TV a year ago. I should have left well alone. I think the committee chairman has left his stamp on this decision.

CULTURAL QUIZ for BRAINWARES

1. In which country does the same motor car cost most and why?
   a) Britain b) Germany c) France
2. What do the letters OAP stand for?
3. What do you know about roads? What sort of road is the
   a) MI? b) AI?
4. Can you imagine what the hard shoulder is in the world of traffic?
5. What's the equivalent of the ADAC organisation in Britain?
6. "Can you give me a sliced?" What is this customer buying?
7. What will you be eating if it's sunny side up?
8. Mrs Thatcher has certainly left her stamp on Britain. What is really meant by this statement?
9. Can you name at least three members of the Royal Family?
10. What's the name of the game where you throw little arrows into a target? It's found in pubs.

PLAYING with WORDS

Ernst has got it wrong again. Can you correct his lines and help him when he can't remember the English word?

Ernst: It's really great to be camping over here in this camping bus. In the moment I feel really relaxed.

Jenny: Yes, but I'm afraid there's no electricity on this campsite.

Ernst: No fear! We won't actually need it for a couple of days. We can use the gas that's (übrig geblieben).

Jenny: Well, we'll certainly have some peace and quiet here. There's no soul around.

Ernst: Yes, I'm sure we'll be (in Ruhe gelassen) here. That's good after all the noise of the city. And some hardship belongs to the sport of camping.

Jenny: To tell the truth there's not much hardship in living in this luxury camper.

TIP of the day

Every country is different. Each one has its plus points and deficits. Including yours. Don't think it should be like it is back home.

14

During his time in England Ernst has rubbed shoulders with the law on several occasions. In this case the adventure is a break-in. He's also called to be a witness on another occasion. And, if I remember well, he had some problems over the documents for his motor car at one time in Hampstead.
We also hear something about the violent society in Britain and get some hints on how to behave.

S THE STORYBOARD

They were sitting together in the Kings Arms, a pub with a fire burning away in the grate. It was warm, although it was dark mid-winter. Jenny and Ernst had settled in. They both spent too much time at work, but they enjoyed themselves in their private life, too. Ernst had noticed a social difference between England and Germany. In England you have more opportunity to meet new people, new acquaintances socially. In a way it's more flexible. Ernst's comment on all this: "When I go out in Germany, I like to be with the people I'm with and I know."

Jenny. "But Ernst, that means you'll never get to know new people, you'll never get new impulses into your life."

"Perhaps I need no new impulses. I have impulses enough[1]."

"Well, I'm shocked. I thought you were open-minded. Don't you want to develop yourself?"

"Naturally[2] I want to. But I wanted to say[3] that you have to know somebody in order to talk to him, about important things."

Jenny was irritated. "Well, we'll have to agree to differ. Do you want another pint?"

"No, let's go home before we have a real argument." The unhappy couple left the lovely pub. They arrived at the cottage. They walked along the side of the house to the kitchen door, which was open.

"My God, we are broken in[4]," Ernst screeched.

"Oh no." Jenny was in tears. "How could that have happened?"

Ernst was beside himself. "I'll say you how[5]. This is a country full of thieves[6]. You can't trust anyone. That's your England[7]."

---

1 I have enough impulses
2 of course
3 I was trying to say
4 we've been broken into
5 I'll tell you how
6 this country's full of thieves
7 that's England for you

14 Ernst phoned the police. The constable was very understanding. "What exactly is missing? Any jewels, money, electrical equipment?" Jenny was confused. "Well, nothing, nothing that I can see." Ernst was grunting like a pig. "No respect for property. A spoilt society[8]."

"Which door did you go out of?" asked the bobby. "The front/the back" (in chorus).

The would-be Sherlock Holmes had got it. "Aha, you went out of two different doors. So who forgot to lock? And who's been wasting the time of the Royal Constabulary?"

A quiet voice in the background. "How could I have locked up? I've never had the key."

LAUGHING at GRAMMAR

Use the correct verb tenses!

a) He knew she __________ (love) antiques, so he gave here an early American washing machine – a tub and a bar of soap.

b) A camper had set up his camp in a national park. He was eating a slice from a bird roasting over a small fire he had lit. A Ranger came by, said hello and then informed him that it __________ (be) a condor. He went on to say that it __________ (be) a protected bird and that he wasn't supposed to kill it. The Ranger warned him that he __________ (can) go to jail for a crime like that. The camper explained it __________ (be) an accident and that his gun __________ (just happen) to go off and that the bird came crashing down. The Ranger said he __________ (will) not fine him in that case and asked him what it __________ (taste) like. The camper replied that it __________ (be) a little like spotted owl.

c) A man believed he was a cannibal so his wife convinced him to go to a psychiatrist. He returned home later and his wife asked him how the psychiatrist __________ (be). The man replied that he __________ (be) delicious.

8 a corrupt society

C CROSSING CULTURES

Crime and society

I must say that there is roughness and violence in the bigger cities in Britain, especially in the Midlands and the North. But, having said that a lot of negative images are generated through the media. Britain's big cities are no worse than others of comparable size in Europe.

There it is, of course, petty theft and mugging especially where five or ten percent of the population have no work. And, it goes without saying, the tourist or the foreigner is the easy target. They wander along, tired with their fat wallets always sticking out of their back pockets or with their handbags on their knees in the tube. It's all asking for trouble. Normally, people with a brain should know better.

In Britain we have about five or six percent of unemployed people (compare with eleven or twelve percent in Germany). It's rather obvious that if the situation allows it, some of these people will do their thing. We do indeed still have our problems with the IRA who place bombs here and there when they think it necessary.

Crime and violent behaviour are often the result of frustration. Perhaps this is why we see violent groups of youths running around smashing things on a Saturday evening. Of course we should all try to understand their anal problems as they shatter our front room windows.

How to avoid trouble

What about a few simple rules for not getting into trouble in England? For example, don't get into an argument with an angry looking youth. If you're travelling by tube in the evening, make sure you sit in a carriage with other people.

Outside in the country the crime rate drops sharply because there is no real market for the criminals. But it can always happen that your cottage is broken into. Do your best to have your things insured. If you are confronted by a robber or something like that, don't play the hero (unless you are fully trained to do so) and keep a cool head!

LAUGHING A LITTLE

There was a serious motorway accident last night when a police van carrying three convicted thieves on their way to prison was in collision with a truck carrying a large load of cement. The prisoners escaped and the police are now looking for three hardened criminals.

There's a permanent crime wave where I live. It's the only place I know that, when you buy a pair of nylon stockings, they ask you for your head size.

A man who has never gone to school may steal from a freight car, but if he has a university education he may steal the whole railroad.
Franklin D. Roosevelt

The police had hired the local village hall to give a talk about crime and other problems in the neighbourhood. The police impressed on all the inhabitants of the village that the community policeman was always available to assist in the prevention of crime and nuisances like children cycling on the pavement.
Thus it was that at 1.00 a.m. the community policeman received a phone call from an elderly man. "I can't sleep for all the noise," he complained.
"What's causing it? Do you want me to make an arrest for breach of the peace?" asked the policeman.
"I don't know. It's two cats mating on the wall outside my house. They're making a hideous racket with all their love calls and things."
"Cats!" exclaimed the policeman. "Why don't you walk up to the cats, give one of them a sharp prod and tell it that he is wanted on the phone?"
"Will that make them stop?"
"It certainly stopped me," said the community policeman, bitterly.

PERFECT your PHRASALS

Here are some more phrasals to help Ernst and perhaps, you.
➜ We've been broken into.

BREAK

break out of (prison)	ausbrechen
break off	abbrechen
break the back of something	das Schlimmste hinter sich bringen
break one's word	das Wort brechen
break all records	alle Rekorde brechen
break a habit	eine Gewohnheit ablegen

LAUGHING A LITTLE

Having friends!

Ernst: I hate moving house. It's so tiring with all the furniture.

Jenny: Come on. If we keep at it all afternoon, we'll break the back of the worst of it today.

Ernst: What do you mean 'we keep at it'? I have to do the heavy work. If I manage to carry all this stuff out today, I'll break all records for weight-lifting.

Jenny: The only thing you'll break is your word. You promised to help me clear it out today and now you say it's too difficult.

Ernst: O.k., O.k.! I don't want to disappoint you and make problems when it's so important for you to get everything moved out by tomorrow. But see if you can stop moaning and complaining, and then you'll be breaking a habit of a lifetime.

14

CULTURAL QUIZ for BRAINWARES

1. What's the name of the false hairpiece that the judges in court wear?
2. How many men and women are there in a jury in Britain?
3. What's a bobby?
4. What's the policeman's patrol area called?
   He has to walk the b____t.
5. A person accused of a crime is innocent until he's proved g_______y.
6. What is the only weapon that a policeman carries in Britain?
7. If you are found guilty in court you may then be
   a) sentenced **b)** acquitted **c)** accused
8. Another way of saying a convicted criminal was put into prison is that he was
   a) sent in **b)** sent up **c)** sent down
9. Who is the head of the police force in Britain?
10. What is the Old Bailey?

PLAYING with WORDS

At the police station. Ernst was a witness to a crime. But he forgot some words and got some others wrong.

Sergeant: So, if you could just describe to me what happened, Mr Lachnit.

Ernst: Yes, sir. I was just coming out of my office when I saw that somebody was trying to break ______ the off-licence on the other side of the road.

Sergeant: What did this individual look like? Can you remember?

Ernst: Naturally! He was very long and good-built. He was weighing about one hundred kilos. He ran out with the money and broke ______ a car at the side of the road. But no fear, I got the car's number.

TIP of the day

Some things are universal, such as crime, police and disappointment. Don't generalise in a negative way about a country. Stand back a bit!

15

Ernst has been at his new company for about a year. The work has gone well and Ernst has become a popular fellow. Now he gets a big break. Let's see how he copes with it.
There is extra information about working practices and attitudes in Britain and Germany.
And, of course, plenty of jokes.

THE STORYBOARD

Ernst and Jenny had been living in Hampstead for just less than a year. "Jesus how the time runs[1]," was Ernst's comment one day to his boss in the engineering office.

"Yes, you're right there," commented Rob Allen. "By the way, it seems, you've been with us for ages. How long has it actually been?"

"A short year. I'm here[2] since December 1999. It was a very interesting period." Rob put his hand on Ernst's shoulder. "There's something I want to talk to you about." Ernst felt uncomfortable. It was only a few months since he had had all that trouble at the party. And there had been several similar occasions. "Perhaps someone had whistled[3]." Ernst turned pale. "It wasn't my guilt[4] in any case."

Rob went on. "We've been watching your case with interest." Ernst's mind was racing. "My work was always good. And I was always the last one to leave the office," he thought to himself. "Ernst, I have to tell you that I'm leaving this subsidiary to go to Spain as Head of Engineering."

"Jesus, who's going to overtake[5] all your work? Things will break together[6] without you." "That's just the point I wanted to talk about. Ernst, the management and myself consider that you would fill this position perfectly. Your work is accurate, well organised and always on time. Are you interested?"

Half an hour later, on the phone. "Jenny Bell, they've promoted me. I'm responsible for the whole engineering division here in England. What for luck[7]!"

A week later Ernst was standing on a platform in front of more than one hundred eager little Englanders. His new responsibility was cross-location. That meant he was in charge of engineers from all the different sites in Britain.

---

1 how time flies
2 I've been here
3 perhaps someone had blown the whistle / denounced him
4 my fault
5 take over
6 will collapse
7 what luck!

15

"Ladies and Gentlemen, First of all I'd like to begin by thanking you for offering your time so late in the afternoon. I know you all work very hard and many hours. This is perhaps part of the reason why the technical side of our products is so well respected. I come to the reason for our gathering today. As you already know I have been offered the job of chief engineer, Britain. Believe me, this was absolute[8] unexpected. But now that I have become accustomed to the idea and the responsibilities of the job I will carry it out to the best of my abilities.

Next, I would like to say a few words to my predecessor, Mr Rob Allen. Rob has run this department for fifteen years, and everybody tells me that nobody could have made a better job of it. Thank-you Rob, for all your efforts. To the rest of you, I'll make it short. Actually I was ordered by several very competent people not to talk too much. Namely by my better half and my squash partner. So I'll do just that. Thank-you for all your support. Keep up the good work! I thank you all."

There were sounds of cheers and comments like, "not bad for a foreigner." Ernst was happy. You may wonder how he managed such a good speech. Answer: together with Jenny over a good bottle of Chianti.

LAUGHING at GRAMMAR

Find the correct preposition!

a) A young woman went _____ a bank and asked to withdraw some money. "Can you identify yourself?" asked the bank clerk. The young woman opened her handbag, took _____ a mirror, looked _____ it and said, "yes, it's me all right."

b) It was the first scheduled passenger flight _____ the moon. The two hundred passengers fastened their seat belts and the gigantic spaceship nosed its way _____ _____ the clouds _____ its far off destination.

8 completely / absolutely

The passengers could hear the soft throbbing _____ the powerful engines and settled _____ in their comfortable seats to enjoy the journey. Then a voice was heard. It said: "Good morning, Ladies and Gentlemen! And a very warm welcome _____ Mini-Moon Trips – and our first scheduled passenger flight _____ the Moon. It may interest you to know that this marvellously designed spaceship has been checked and double checked; and to eliminate the chance of any human errors the spaceship is completely crewed _____ robots; so rest assured, Ladies and Gentlemen, nothing _____ all can go wrong ... can go wrong ... can go wrong."

C CROSSING CULTURES

Comparing working life

There are certainly some differences in the working environment between the British and the German. The author allows himself a comparison as he has lived and worked for long periods in both countries. Of course, comments will be some sort of generalisations since they are based on personal experience.

In Britain, for example, it seems that employees and companies in general have a lighter attitude to work. Perhaps they do not take it so seriously as in Germany. There is more socialising, such as in the ways mentioned earlier in this book – the one for the road, office parties, drink after work together etc. The atmosphere at work is lighter. This may be interpreted as "muddling through", as not being strictly organised.

Experiences in Germany show a stronger needs for analysis, processes and targets. There is more monitoring of everything. Things seem to be more organised. Germans would argue that all this is necessary. They even have an expression for it: "Trusting is good, but checking it is better."

In offices and companies in Britain the employees will normally use first names with each other, even with the boss. This does not mean that everybody is "per du" with each other and that there are any special or unusual relationships in the pipeline. As mentioned in an earlier chapter it might be in Germany the "Erich, Sie" situation. In general, though, the atmosphere is not as formal as in Germany, at least on the surface.

Regarding the hierarchy of levels, little boss, bigger boss, biggest boss, I wanted to say that this is more marked in Germany, but to tell the truth it my be easier to identify in Germany, though it is also present in Britain. Perhaps it is more hidden and therefore even more difficult to deal with than in Germany. And this author has the feeling that class and old boys' networks still play too much of a role in Britain. In Germany this is replaced by a "kumpelhaft" technical approach to the things. It's difficult to put one's finger on all these things.

Britain is more of a meritocracy. If you're good at you things, there at the right time and place, you'll probably get the job. In Germany it's different. Firstly, society is split into two serious parts – private industry and the state sector. In the state sector you have the civil servants (Beamte etc.). Here no foreigner can be involved. The private sector could employ foreigners and does, but for important jobs they normally take Germans. This thinking is changing as German companies go global. In the last five or ten years the Germans are taking the best man for the job, too.

In Britain this process started earlier, but who knows what the English really think about it?

Anyway Ernst has profited from this trend. By the way this author also works in Germany on a permanent basis and that speaks volumes, too.

LAUGHING A LITTLE

Jenny: What time does your secretary start work?
Ernst: About two hours after she gets there.

The longer the title, the less important the job.

An executive is someone who can take three hours for lunch without hindering production.

A successful manager is one who believes in sharing the credit with the man who did the work.

A consultant is someone who's brought in at the last minute to share the blame.

PERFECT your PHRASALS

And the story goes on.
→ I will carry it out.

CARRY

carry the can	die Verantwortung tragen
carry the day	einen Sieg landen
(be) carried away	begeistert (sein)
carry on (with)	weitermachen mit
carry out	umsetzen, verwirklichen

LAUGHING A LITTLE

The soft touch!

Boss: Carry on with your work, you men. I want you to be finished by the weekend.

Worker: Oh, crikey! I think that's going too far. We would need to work at least ten hours a day.

Boss: I'm not here to discuss these things with you. You will carry out my instructions! Or else I'm going to fire you all.

Tradė Unionist: O.k., boys! We'd better do as he says or he'll get carried away with visions of his own power.

CULTURAL QUIZ for BRAINWARES

1. What are the two names for the boss in a limited and public limited company?
2. Ernst got a better job with more money. Let's hope he will enjoy his p__________.
3. Somebody wanted to blow the whistle on Ernst. Can you explain what this really means?
4. In Britain we have a very rigid top-down hierarchy. What do we mean by 'top-down' here?
5. Which organisation in Britain is supposed to represent the interests of the workers?
6. What name do we give to that strange British habit of standing in lines waiting for things?
7. What's the meaning of "going Dutch"?
8. What about some more opposites?
   a) marriage =
   b) death =
   c) age =
   d) House of Lords =

PLAYING with WORDS

Ernst has formulated some sentences but he forgets bits.

a) I've been here a year already. How time __________!

b) There was a big problem at work because of a mistake in the sales department. The boss was furious. I'm glad it wasn't my __________.

c) The boss has __________ me to Head of Engineering.

d) It's a lot of responsibility. I hope I can carry __________ my tasks successfully.

e) You'd better do, Ernst, because as the boss you carry the __________ in the end.

f) Carry ________ ______ the good work, Ernst!

TIP of the day

Don't be afraid to accept a challenge. Remember, it's different from back home. You might even do better.

16

Here we see our hero being initiated into the habit of socialising in the company. Even as the boss he has some other responsibilities to ensure that his team functions well. And even in the best planned events things can go wrong.
A description of the world of television is also included as this plays such a dominant role in the private lives of most people.

THE STORYBOARD

Time passed. Ernst was enjoying his new responsibilities as Head of Engineering and it was generally agreed that he was doing a good job. It was coming up to Christmas again. It was actually the beginning of December. Dan Johnson, the assistant Head of Engineering was sitting next to Ernst in the canteen. "Don't you think it's time we organised the office party for the last week before Christmas?"

"Dan, you're a genie[1]. I'd completely forgotten about that. As I was[2] engineer in Germany the parties were always managed by the secretaries." Dan smiled. "That's a bit old-fashioned, isn't it? Ladies cooking in the kitchen."

"Hmm, perhaps it is. Okay, what will be the best date for it?" Dan suggested the 24th of December at four in the afternoon. Ernst couldn't believe his ears. "Back in Germany we always have the party in office time and often some time before Christmas." Dan was adamant. "No, it has to come more or less at the end before the holiday. Imagine they all turned up the day after to work with bad hangovers. There wouldn't be any work done."

"Is it the same practice with all our concurrence[3] here?"

"The same everywhere."

Ernst remembered he had seen a TV documentary film about British work practices. "Yes, I watched a film in TV[4] which showed the long hours they sometimes work in England. In my meaning[5] in some ways working conditions are not as good as they are in Germany. But on the other side[6] perhaps we have too many rights over there. Nowadays we can't afford so many social benefits. Okay, let's get down to the planning."

Three weeks later the office party was in full swing in the canteen. Ernst had really gone to town on this task. His secretary, Ellen, was chattering to him. "I'm really surprised you organised so much alcohol for the staff. We didn't expect it."

---

1 a genius
2 when I was
3 competition
4 on TV
5 in my opinion
6 on the other hand

16

"As we say when we do it then we do it[7]. I know English people prefer ales like Guinness, and lagers and bitters, so I ordered a barrel of each." "Anyway," smiled Ellen, staggering into Ernst's arms (she was somewhat blue[8]), "anyway, I'm really happy you've brought your continental ways to us. It's much more interesting." Ernst had a red face as he struggled to disentangle himself from Ellen's grip. At that moment who should come through the door of the canteen but Jenny? Ernst, totally uncomfortable, "Hi, I wasn't awaiting you[9]. Shouldn't you be at work?"

"I see you weren't expecting me. I think I'll just go right back where I came from. Good-bye."

LAUGHING at GRAMMAR

Let's check out verb tenses!

a) If I _________ (know) how old I was going to get, I'd have taken much better care of myself.

b) If you don't learn from your mistakes, what _________ (be) the point in making them?

c) They offered me a raise if I _________ (work) hard. I knew there was a catch there somewhere.

d) Remember, if there had never been any lawyers, there _________ (never be) any need for them.

e) You _________ (know) you're overweight when you can't get you and the water into the bath at the same time.

7 in for a penny, in for a pound 8 drunk / merry 9 expecting you

C CROSSING CULTURES

The importance of television

Well, after that office party Ernst decided to go home and watch the telly. Since we've talked about parties and so on, we'll take this opportunity to look at TV in England.

Of course, TV is everywhere. One in four children has his own TV set, and an average each child spends thirteen hours a week in front of it. And after 9 p.m. many children get the chance to watch sex, violence and sordid things. The situation is made worse by the huge number of satellite channels in addition to the regular four or five terrestrial broadcasters.

BBC 1 and BBC 2 are still non-commercial which means we all have to pay a licence for them. ITV, Channel 4 and 5 are overgrown with advertising spots.

Commercials. These slots appearing on the independent channels have developed a genre of their own. They are often more interesting than the programmes that they interrupt. Frequently the stars of the ads are also the stars of the programmes themselves, just earning extra money in their spare time.

Documentaries. Britain is a leader in producing this type of information film. They are especially well-known for their wild-life and ecology films. These documentaries are famous internationally. Do you remember the three part-series of *Running with the Dinosaurs* about one year ago? The film caused an uproar because of its daring comments. Highly entertaining.

However, our Ernst, when he arrived back at the cottage after the office party was more likely to have watched a sitcom or a soap opera. These events seem to attract most of the population. Sitcoms last half an hour, give information about all classes or levels in society and can be extremely funny or very boring.

Soap operas have become an institution. Some of them have been running for years. I remember *Coronation Street* back in the sixties. Now there are soaps originating in different regions of England. The above-mentioned soap is located in the English Midlands, the *Eastenders* shows the East End, a poorer part of London. And there are others. What they all have in common is they show underlying aggression (just look at the faces of the characters) and deal with family crises. They're not light, but when you've watched for a couple you start to identify and even look forward to the main protagonists.

Big Brother. This new internationally successful series comes from so-called Reality TV. Invented in Holland, it involves locking ten or more people in a house and watching them behave or misbehave. Then, we the viewers, have the right to eliminate one of the participants every week or so. The little Englanders go even further. In addition they dumped fifty people on an uninhabited island a year ago to see how they would manage with each other under hard conditions. This island is off the west coast of Scotland.

All that apart, I'm pretty sure Ernst was watching the sitcom, *Steptoe and Son*, about two scrap-merchants and their problems in life.

LAUGHING A LITTLE

I watched a thought-provoking programme on television last night.
The thought it provoked was, "Why am I watching this programme?"

The way things are going, people will soon start demanding longer commercials.

Our local TV weatherman is so bad,
he couldn't even predict yesterday's weather.

A lot of today's shows are what they call reality shows.
They show murders, assaults, cops breaking into homes.
In my neighbourhood, you just have to look out the window.

Television takes our minds off our minds.

PERFECT your PHRASALS

Ernst fights his phrasals again.

➜ It was coming up to Christmas.

COME

come about	geschehen
come across	stoßen auf
come of	"werden aus"
come over	in jemanden gefahren sein, "etwas haben"
come to	wieder zu sich kommen

LAUGHING A LITTLE

A strange event in the Amazon!

Interviewer: Your expedition to the Amazon has not been very successful, has it? Can you tell us how it all came about? Would you explain to us what came of your plans to camp in an Indian village?

Explorer: Well, you're right. We had some trouble. When we first entered the village we came across a strange statue of a god standing next to the main gate. We thought we were going to be really lucky, but at the same time most of us felt an unpleasant depressing feeling coming over us.

Interviewer: And what happened during the night?

Explorer: That's when it all went wrong. I heard a noise. I got up to investigate. Suddenly I felt a terrific pain in my head. I fell down on the floor, unconscious. When I came to several hours later all the other members of the expeditions had disappeared. Their clothes were lying there untouched.

CULTURAL QUIZ for BRAINWARES

1. What is perhaps the most popular town for summer holidays and beach in England?
2. In the nineteenth century the capital, London, was often covered with a sort of industrial fog caused by burning brown coal. What was this phenomenon called?
3. What's the name of the new Reality TV series called where people are watched twenty-four hours a day?
4. What's Balmoral Castle?
5. There is a region in north-west England which is full of lakes. What is it called?
6. What are the two most famous "soaps" in Britain?
7. What is the name given to an advertising slot on TV?
8. Which sport has one of its most famous competitions at St. Andrews?
9. Which sport has one of its most famous competitions at Lords?
10. What's a Morgan +6?

PLAYING with WORDS

Ernst needs some help with his translations.

Sehr geehrte Damen und Herren!
Ich möchte mich für Ihr heutiges Erscheinen bedanken. Ich komme direkt zum Punkt. Unsere Konkurrenten werden sehr aktiv. Meiner Meinung nach müssen wir uns dagegen wehren. Ich glaube, das bedeutet, dass wir eine Fernsehkampagne starten müssen. Damit erreichen wir viele Menschen. Andererseits ist diese Art von Werbung sehr teuer. Auf jeden Fall bin ich mir sicher, dass etwas aus diesem Projekt wird.
Vielen Dank.

TIP of the day

You can learn a lot from TV and radio. For info listen to Radio 4. It'll tell you what's going on in the world. World Service MW 648.

17

Ernst is fighting with a problem most of us have experienced. Eating too much, drinking too much, doing too little exercise and not moving our bodies.
Result: our trousers don't fit any longer. Bottom line, depression. He discusses this matter with the ever slim Jenny.
The extra information deals with eating, wrong-doings or wrong-eatings, a bit about health. But Ernst has it all in grip[1].

1 under control

THE STORYBOARD

Of course, Ernst had got a taste for those real ales, especially the dark heavy ones that are full of calories. And he was into Indian curry. "I like the convenience of the takeaways." All that together with the fact that he couldn't do any sport. He was limping along after his operation for the torn cartilage on the knee. The result of it all was that he put on a lot of weight. More than a stone which means seven or eight kilos. So Jenny, who had remained as slim as a rake, decided to take action. "It's time you did something about it. You're as flabby as a pudding."

"Oh, don't say that. I'm just a little strongly built." Jenny wasn't having any of it. "You eat too much per day. You don't train. Your calorie intake is more than 3,000 a day, and the bottom line is you're getting fat. And I don't like fat men." Ernst who felt this was all a little bit unfair began to defend himself. "Okay, okay, I'll start to make a diet[2]. And I'll start jogging again, even if it kills me."

"Oh, don't make us feel sorry for you. You've got to change your life style, your habits."

"Alright. I'll do it. I'll eliminate all my junk food like fizzy drinks and hamburgers. But I tell you! Life will not be worth to live[3]. I'll be a skeleton. And I work hardly[4]. I'll have nothing from my life. When I come home I need something nice. I grant myself nothing else[5]."

"Have you quite finished? Should we all break out in tears? Is that what you want? You've got to be positive. Think positive! Listen, I've got just the thing for a lazy fellow like you. It's called the Scarsdale diet."

Ernst was a bit suspicious. "I don't trust diets. You cut down on everything. You lose weight. Then you eat more and then you take to[6]. It doesn't work. How long does it exist for[7], this Scarsdale diet?" "Oh, don't be so negative. People started using it in the sixties. The idea is to cut out all fat and sugar. So no beer or wine. And you can eat your normal quantities of food, so no yo-yo effect. You should separate your food, so don't

2 go on a diet
3 worth living
4 I work hard
5 I've no other pleasures in life
6 put on weight
7 How long has it existed?

mix carbohydrates with vegetables." Ernst had become interested. "It's like our Trennkost." You can eat potatoes and meat, but you should eat them separately. Okay, let's try it, but remember, like everything else in life, we shouldn't overdrive[8]. When do we start?"

LAUGHING at GRAMMAR

Preposition workshop!

a) A car is a four-wheeled vehicle that runs _______ hills and _______ pedestrians.

b) I don't understand. Why do they call it the "rush hour" when everything is _______ a standstill?

c) Everything I cook turns _______ tough. Can anybody lend me a soup knife?

d) I'm determined to stay _______ _______ debt, even if I have to borrow money to do it.

e) A refrigerator is the place where you keep leftovers _______ they are ready to be thrown _______ .

f) My wife was furious _______ me because I came home late _______ a New Year's Eve party – _______ August.

8 we shouldn't exaggerate

C CROSSING CULTURES

Unhealthy lifestyle

In the western world most of us have a problem to keep the pounds off. What do they say? "An adult is someone who's stopped growing at both ends and started growing in the middle." The reasons are mixed. On the one hand we eat more than our daily intake of 2,000 to 3,000 calories per day. At the same time we take less exercise and travel more by car. At the end of the day, in the evening we stuff ourselves full and fall into bed with this extra two kilos, probably experiencing a troubled sleep.

Next comes the type or quality of the food we put inside us. It can be that in countries like Portugal with huge supplies of fresh fish, tomatoes and olive oil, where the fish is grilled often in the open air, that the population is well nourished. But in countries like Britain or Germany a lot of the food is fried, or large portions of meat are served up with dollops of fattening sauces and gravies. Large portions are ladled out on every plate. Salad and fruit definitely takes a back seat. And calories dance on the grave of our slim figures!

Looking at Britain, you can buy high quality raw materials, salads, tomatoes and you can cook marvellously inside your own four walls. But this all needs time and our modern little Englanders don't have time, or prefer to spend it on more mundane matters like an after-work drink with colleagues. So most people eat in pubs or get takeaways. Be sure about one thing! All those foods are cooked in old oils. Absolute freshness was not the priority.

What have we got in this type of food? It begins with the bread. Your average loaf in England is some sort of soft rubbery bread. In most cases this is refined, so it's not good for the digestion. Then we go on to steaks and pies of a thousand sorts, Yorkshire pudding etc. A lot of tasty things and a tyre around the waist. What do they say?

"Everything you like makes you fat!"

LAUGHING A LITTLE

He'd be the perfect weight for his height
if he were three metres and thirty.

It's depressing – the only thing about me
that's getting thinner is my hair.

I knew it was time to go on a diet when the airline
made me pay excess baggage on my own body.

On his latest diet, my husband is losing two kilos a week.
In a year and a half I'll be rid of him completely.

PERFECT your PHRASALS

Welcome to the phrasal corner again.
→ You cut down on everything.

CUT

cut back on	kürzen, reduzieren
cut out	vermeiden, aufgeben
cut corners	die Sache abkürzen
cut one's losses	die Verluste abschreiben

LAUGHING A LITTLE

A starvation diet!

Linda: I'm overweight! I'm going to cut down on my food by a half. I also need to cut back on my expenses.

Andy: I don't think it'll help. You need to do some sport.

Linda: Why? You know that I'm an active sort of person.

Andy: Active? The only active thing about you is your imagination. If you take my advice you'll cut out food completely. That might help.

CULTURAL QUIZ for BRAINWARES

1. How many kilos is ten stone?
2. What's the name of the medical service in Britain?
3. When you go to live somewhere in Britain as soon as you have a fixed address, you should r____________ with a doctor.
4. What do we call it when you give yourself medicine instead of going to the doctor?
5. Which type of school would you have to pay school fees for?
   a) secondary **b)** public **c)** private
6. What is the type of school called where the pupils sleep at the school during the term?
   a) internat **b)** boarding school **c)** dormitory
7. Which examination in Britain is equivalent to the German "Abitur"?
8. Who is the religious head of the Church of England?
9. A little geography. What are the three main seas surrounding Britain?
10. A little more difficult. There is an island off the coast of west Scotland. It is also famous for its wool which is mostly made into white pullovers or sweaters. What's the name?

17

PLAYING with WORDS

Find Ernst's mistakes. Correct them!

Ernst: Jenny, I know you have complained about my weight. Anyhow, I've made diet in the last three weeks.

Jenny: Well, what was the result of that?

Ernst: You won't believe it but I have taken off two kilos. I'm getting as thin as a beanstalk.

Jenny: Yes, you look better. How did you do it?

Ernst: Well, I *vermied* all sorts of fried food, beer and *Fett*. And I've taken up jogging and swimming again.

Jenny: Go for it, Ernst!

TIP of the day

Trying to keep fit? Go to a leisure centre. They have weight training, squash, swimming, etc. They are in every little town in Britain. But watch out! Brits are conservative. Bathers must be worn in saunas. Strange lot, aren't they?

18

In this episode Ernst encounters the British pastime of doing good deeds. This often means going against the government. It can involve participation in demonstrations. Information is given on how these activities are carried out in Britain.

Ernst is really integrating, isn't he?

18

S THE STORYBOARD

As I mentioned before Jenny and Ernst had rented a lovely little old cottage which had been built in the Middle Ages. As you all know, it is located in Hamstead, North London. It is a village in its own right, with a village green and a little lake at the top of the road. A beautiful, peaceful place. And then it happened. Ernst was talking to the baker in the corner shop.

"I suppose you've heard the news, Mr Lachnit." Ernst was intrigued. "Which news are they[1], Mr Burnitt? Politic[2], the government, another stupid law?"

"Nobody's interested in all that stuff. No, this is much more serious. Do you want your normal brown granary loaf by the way?" "Of course. You know I don't like white sliced bread. In Germany we name it[3] 'rubber bread'."

The baker kept his usual good humour. "One man's meat is another man's poison. Anyway, as I was saying there's some news. They're going to build an incineration plant at the top of the road near your cottage. Just five hundred yards away to be exact." "An incineration plant? What's that? Some sort of a garden?" The baker was amused. "Ha ha. It's not for growing things. More for burning things. The only thing that will grow is the pollution in the air."

Ernst had got it at last. "You mean a combustion plant[4]. For burning waste. My God, near our cottage. It'll stink[5] terribly."

The baker agreed. "You're right. It'll affect the whole village. We've got to take action."

Ernst felt his blood was beginning to boil. "I didn't believe it at first, but I must say I heard something about it while a meeting[6] at work. We should undertake something as quick as it goes[7]."

"What do you want to do? What can we do?" Mr Burnitt was surprised how motivated Ernst was. "We should avoid to allow[8] the inhabitants of

1 which news is that
2 politics
3 we call it
4 incineration plant
5 it'll smell terribly / terrible
6 during a meeting
7 do something as soon as possible
8 we should avoid allowing

the village to sit around and turn their thumbs[9]. I must make me on the socks[10]. I have things to do."

At the hospital in the nurses' rest room the telephone rang impatiently. After a while a passing nurse lifted the receiver. Guess who it was!

"Hello Jenny here. Can I help you?" "Hi Jenny. It's Ernst. There's a problem. You mustn't worry about it now, but we need a strategy."

Jenny began to get nervous. "Just what's happened? What's going on? You sound completely upset." "No problem, no problem. It's just that we must organise a letter. They're burning waste outside our window."

"Who's burning waste?" "The government. The council." Jenny saw the light. "Oh, an incinerator. Well, you're right. We should start a petition today. Listen, what you have to do first is ..."

LAUGHING at GRAMMAR

Those tricky Conditional Sentences!

a) My wife, besides being rather fat, is incredibly bossy – always telling people what they should do. One day she was on a bus and had just settled down and got comfortable in her seat when she saw that the only standing passengers were three middle-aged women.

My wife turned to the man sitting next to her and said in a very loud voice: "If you __________ (be) a gentleman, you'd get up and __________ (let) one of those women sit down."

"If you were a lady," said the man, "you __________ (get) up and let all three of them sit down."

b) Teacher: "If I __________ (be) to ask you to add 8,569 to 359 and then halve it, what do you think you __________ (get)?"
Jimmy: "The wrong answer, sir."

9 twiddling their thumbs 10 I've got to get a move on

c) If the bride ___________ (wear) white for her wedding as a symbol of purity and joy – then why does the groom always wear the opposite, black?

C CROSSING CULTURES

Doing good deeds

A lot of people in Britain simply get on with their lives quietly no matter what happens. But even on the island we have a minority of highly motivated people who take up the banner when they feel that some unjust or unfair situation is happening. Those unfair situations could include a whole series of issues. We might mention, for example, the fact that bad old local government or central government comes along and has plans to cut down some ancient trees, dig up a park, run a motorway through your garden, put a nuclear power plant next to your village or establish an incineration plant outside your town.

On the surface the reasons for doing all these things are always good. It's when you look into the detail that you find there are personal and often financial interests that are playing a role. These incentives soon leak out and it is at this point that our social consciences begin to move. More precisely some people form action or pressure groups, and print their leaflets. They distribute the information by any means they can, sticking it in shop windows and through letter boxes, and everything in order to move large sections of the community to take action. This action may include petitions involving thousands of signatures, or commissioning lawyers to find loop holes in the rules.

Often these initiatives are successful causing some process to grind to a halt. Perhaps one of the most infamous concerned Margaret Thatcher's poll tax. This was a tax per capita on each individual living in a given house. It placed an unbearable load on families. It seems to be a modern government tactic to burden citizens with a multiplicity of hidden taxes. It's surely no accident that we have the highest fuel taxes in the European Union.

LAUGHING A LITTLE

Jill: Do you think voters are apathetic?
Jean: I don't care.

The Englishman is very fond of animals
– especially roasted with two veg.

We started this charity just three weeks ago and already we've raised nearly £ 100,000 – and we haven't even got a disease yet.

A philanthropist is a person who gives away publicly the fortune he stole privately.

PERFECT your PHRASALS

➜ The inhabitants of the village sat around.

SIT

sit back	in Ruhe abwarten
sit it out	durchhalten
sit up straight	gerade sitzen
sit on the fence	neutral bleiben
sit pretty	es gut haben

LAUGHING A LITTLE

Hunger a mile high

Freddy: Phew! I really don't like flying. It makes me nervous. But I guess I'll just have to sit it out. It'll be over soon.

Egbert: Try to relax. Just sit back and don't think about it.

Freddy: Well, the stewardess told me I should sit up straight so that I can eat the food they are serving. And I don't want to miss that. Flying might kill me one way or another but it won't kill my appetite.

18 CULTURAL QUIZ for BRAINWARES

1. What's the name of the famous British international radio (and now TV) news service?
2. Remember that clock in London on the bank of the Thames? What's it called?
3. There is a range of hills that separate Scotland from England. What is its name?
4. Where are the Orkneys located and what are they?
5. What's the function of a town-crier?
6. Which well-known game was based on buying and selling houses on the streets of London?
7. Where have nearly all English monarchs been crowned?
8. What is Sir Christopher Wren's masterpiece?
9. Where are the Crown Jewels housed?
10. Who are the guardians of the King's buffet?

PLAYING with WORDS

Correct Ernst's mistakes

1. At the restaurant:

Ernst: Hmmm. Something smells well here. What is it?
Waiter: That's the venison pie, sir.
Ernst: Well, I certainly take that. And could I have a bottle of red wine while the meal, with the main course.
Waiter: Certainly, sir.
Ernst: Well, Jenny, we are going well since I got my promotion. We name that really good luck!

2. Find words for these definitions:

a) a list of signatures =
b) to give an order or job to =
c) opposite of majority =

TIP of the day

Shops are normally open after 9 a.m. If you need something in the evening, go to an off-licence. Dont go to a petrol station for alcohol. You won't get any.

19

Ernst has to learn it, too. You don't fool around with the blue bottles (a slang name for our trusted and trusting defenders of the law). There we see the bureaucratic side of the matter. There are rules and regulations everywhere.

In addition we try to give you a feeling of how the people see authority and what their attitude is to law and order.

S THE STORYBOARD

Of course, as we all know Ernst is a social creature and he takes his responsibilities seriously. In the last chapter we saw that he was pretty involved in those anti-incinerator activities, to halt the development of the plant. They stuck posters on everybody's doors and windows saying "Don't burn your waste in our back garden!" Yes, our heroes fought on with their campaign. But our Ernst was becoming known. It started with his nice BMW motor car. The police stopped him in Hamstead. (Actually it was the police from Central London somewhere, or so Ernst thought.)

They pulled Ernst over to the side of the road. Our hero was upset. "I haven't the palest mould[1] why you've stopped my car."

"Just routine, sir. We've seen your car around this area quite a few times. Does the vehicle belong to you?" Feeling annoyed Ernst replied, "it certainly does and I've paid for it, too."

"We're sure you have, sir, and I'm equally sure you've got the documents for the vehicle with you. Could I see them, please?" Ernst was beginning to lose his temper. "Really, you're wasting much of my time[2]. Of course I have everything. Please[3]!" (Normally Ernst's English is much better, but he had become completely upset with the whole thing.)

"Okay, that seems to be fine. When did you arrive in England, by the way?" With relief, Ernst, "Oh, about eighteen months ago. I work here." "Oh, so you're resident, so to speak?"

"I certainly am. I pay my taxes all five minutes[4] like every Englishman. But independent from that[5] I like it here. England's not the worst[6]. The policeman scratched his head. "Thank you for your observations, sir. By the way, you're still carrying your German number plates. I think we've got a problem here." "I'm sure I don't know what you mean." "Ignorance is no excuse. You were obliged to change to UK number plates, especially for insurance and tax purposes. I think you'd better present yourself at Hampstead Police Station. We'll take it from there."

1 the least idea
2 a lot of my time
3 here you are!
4 every five minutes
5 apart from that
6 There are worse places than England.

19 Well, all that was a month ago. Today, Ernst had organised a demonstration against the incinerator. Cars were blocking the street. Ernst was in form. He had a loudspeaker. "Well, we citizens can't accept what this government is doing, or[7]?"

A police car drew up beside Ernst. "Excuse me, sir, I think I know you. Ah yes, I remember. The illegal immigrant."

"Apology, what[8]?"

"Nothing, but mark my words, sir, we don't need your sort here!"

LAUGHING at GRAMMAR

Let's check our verb tenses!

a) Four-year-old Jenny: Mummy, can you buy me a metal detector, please?
Mother: Why you __________ (want) one?
Jenny: I'm hoping __________ (find) daddy's watch with it?
Mother: I didn't know daddy __________ (lose) his watch.
Jenny: He hasn't. But I was hoping if I __________ (have) a metal detector and it (pick) up where daddy's watch __________ (be) buried that it would also show me where I've buried daddy in the sand.

b) The young businessman __________ (just set) up on his own and, sitting in his brand-new office on the first morning, he __________ (hear) something coming up the stairs. Determined to give the impression of a go-ahead company, he __________ (pick) up the phone as the visitor entered the office and pretended to __________ (discuss) a million-pound deal.
Finally, after five minutes of high-powered negotiation on contracts and profits etc., he put down the phone.
"Sorry about that. Can I help you?"
And the visitor ________ (say), "Sure, I've come to connect the phone."

7 Can we? 8 Excuse me, what did you say?

C CROSSING CULTURES

Authorities in Britain

The British are a strange lot. Perhaps they are suffering from a sort of national schizophrenia – split personality. It goes through many things. For example, attitude to authorities. On the one hand Brits like to be wild and uncontrolled. They don't like to accept formalities in some situations. Try to get some of them to sign a rental contract for a flat or even a job. A few of them are always seeking ways to avoid responsibility. On the other hand others are very formal and want everything done to the letter of the law.

We saw this in the attitude of the police concerning Ernst's car. The police wanted his documentation in absolutely perfect order. But then again they would say "bring your documents to the police station within three days." That's all and you're expected to do it. It's a strange mixture of strictness together with a relaxed attitude.

Drink and driving is another area where there is really no flexibility at all. If you're over the limit which is low in England, you will "lose" your licence for a year. And that is bad news because it's difficult to pass the test in the first place. There is less theory than in Germany, but more emphasis on the practical side. It often happens that you have to take the test four or five times. You are not allowed any mistake.

LAUGHING A LITTLE

If you can't get a lawyer who knows the law,
get one who knows the judge.

Policeman: You've been found guilty of not stopping at a red light. Do you have anything to say in mitigation?

Ernst: Well, I've often stopped at green lights when I didn't have to.

I was walking home the other day when this man emerged from the shadows. "Sir," he said, "could you please spare me the price of a meal? I've no money, no home, I've no job. All I have in the world is this double-edged knife."

PERFECT your PHRASALS

I have nothing to say you don't know already.
➜ They pulled Ernst over.

PULL

pull out	herausfahren
pull over	heranfahren
pull up (1)	zum Stehen kommen
pull up (2)	zurechtweisen
pull somebody's leg	jemanden durch den Kakao ziehen
pull one's socks up	sich (gehörig) am Riemen reißen

LAUGHING A LITTLE

Happy Christmas

Ken: (at the traffic light)
Look! There's a police car pulling up next to us. What do they want?

Driver: (of police car)
Would you mind pulling your car over to the side of the road after the traffic lights?

Ken: Well, I'm sure I don't know what I've done, officer.

Driver: I've been following your car for ten minutes now. There is a list of things. First, you pulled out of a side street without stopping and nearly caused an accident. Second, you drove through red lights. And if I'm not mistaken I can smell alcohol on your breath.

Ken: Hey, you can't pull me up for that. It's Christmas!

Driver: Blow into this breathalyser! You may have to spend your Christmas Day in our company at the police station.

CULTURAL QUIZ for BRAINWARES

1. What do you need to drive legally on public roads in Britain?
2. What is a truncheon?
3. What do we call a permit to drive a car?
4. What's a Nummernschild in English?
5. What's the name of the constitution in England?
6. What's an estate agent?
   a) a manager of the lord's land
   b) a man who buys and sells houses for others
   c) a man who buys and sells shares (Aktien)
7. Who would you entrust with your financial problems?
   a) tax advisor b) lawyer c) investor
8. You've been accused of stealing. Who do you want to defend you?
   a) Queen's Council b) defender c) defence council

19 PLAYING with WORDS

Translate the German, correct the mistakes.

Ernst is driving. He goes down a one-way street by accident.

Policeman: (waving at Ernst)
Could you (heranfahren), please? Now then, sir. What do you think you're doing?

Ernst: I haven't the (geringste Idee) what you're talking about. What have I done wrong?

Policeman: You're driving the wrong way down a one-way street.

Ernst: You (ziehen mich durch den Kakao). I didn't see a sign. I'm not from here, you know.

Policeman: You'd better (sich am Riemen reißen) or there'll be problems.

Ernst: Hmmm. England's not the worst.

TIP of the day

In the case of emergency, robbery, accident, crime, etc., phone 999. For operator enquiries, phone 192.

Just as in Germany various celebrations take place in Britain, too. In their details they are different in the two countries. Ernst gets to know some of these variation in his time in England.

In addition to all that you get some extra information about other celebrations.

20

S THE STORYBOARD

Time flies. Although Ernst had already spent a Christmas in England this was the first time he had really experienced it. This year he was to enjoy the festive days with Jenny's family! The famous in-laws! It was the 24th December. Here they are at home. Jenny's mother and father are very friendly people. Ernst sat down next to the open fire. Jenny's parents' house was a large one and had been built in the last five years. Suddenly the door bell rang. Ernst opened it. Before him stood some friends of Jenny's mum and dad. They had arranged to go to a pub together to meet some other friends. Sitting in front of the fire with Jenny, Ernst felt he needed to say something. "Your parents are very sympathetic[1], but on the Holy Evening[2] the family should be at home together alone." "Pardon?" Jenny was surprised. "What's wrong?" "I know I'm born[3] in Germany and every country has its own customs but on the 24th December everybody should rather[4] stay together at home."

In an impatient voice Jenny informed Ernst that she and Ernst were also going out to meet some friends of their own. "That's what we do at Christmas!" Our Ernst felt annoyed (as usual). And out they went. Actually, to tell the truth Ernst enjoyed himself quite a lot and met some interesting people. He also felt better when later in the evening Jenny's parents joined Jenny's group of friends for a talk and a night-cap at the Old Squirrel, a fifteenth century inn.

On the twenty-fifth, Christmas Day, Ernst woke up in the morning to find Jenny and her parents grinning at him from the doorway. "Is there something? What's loose[5]?" "Get up, you lazy bones and look into your stocking." "Stocking? I don't wear stockings, only socks, and why should I look into them? And I'm not a lazy dog[6]!" "No, the Christmas stocking." Then Ernst got the message. He saw a long net stocking full of presents. He had put his presents for everybody underneath the

1 nice; friendly
2 Christmas Eve
3 I was born
4 should; ought to
5 Is there anything wrong? What's wrong?
6 a lazy bones

Christmas tree as it belongs[7]. But these strange island people open them on the 25th. Well, our hero had a good morning.

At lunch-time the family drove off to an old pub in the countryside where they enjoyed Christmas dinner. They overfed on turkey, roast potatoes, peas, carrots and broccoli and brown gravy. Afterwards Ernst consumed two portions of Christmas pudding with custard. "My God, I'm so what from blown up[8]. I'll never do this again." That evening Jenny drove back to Hampstead with Ernst sitting next to here happily clutching a bottle of French Pernod to help his digestion.

I'm sure we're all looking forward to more adventures of Ernst Lachnit. "Till soon[9]."

LAUGHING at GRAMMAR

And finally a mixed bag.

a) __________ Christmas, my father crossed a turkey ______________ a centipede so everyone could have a drumstick.

b) If you don't learn __________ your mistakes, what's the point __________ making them?

c) I've decided _____ my New Year's resolution: _______________ the beginning _____ February, I'm resolving not to procrastinate.

d) The ____________ (old) you get the _________ (loud) your snoring becomes. Fortunately, your spouse's hearing deteriorates at the same rate.

e) "The reason you are so fat," pronounced the psychiatrist, "is that your whole life is oriented towards ____________ (eat) and ____________ (drink). You like parties for the starters. A football match to you means hot dogs and beer. ___________ (watch) television is a long succession of snacks. And ..."

7 as one should; like you normally do
8 I'm totally full; I'm completely stuffed
9 See you later

"Wait a minute," interrupted the patient. "Don't you serve anything during psychoanalysis?"

f) I'm going to speak and hopefully you're going to listen, and if you should finish before I do, you'll raise your hand, ________ ______?

g) If you think there's too much government now, just _________ (think) what it __________ (be) like if we __________ (get) as much as we're paying for.

C CROSSING CULTURES

Customs and Celebrations

The British, especially in the countryside, still celebrate some festivals. As we saw from Ernst's experience with Jenny, Christmas is still alive albeit it in a more commercialised form.

Christmas: We saw in the dialogue that Christmas Eve only plays a secondary role, an evening out for a drink. The 25th of December is the main day, and it is a day of stuffing oneself full.

Boxing Day: 26th of December, is also an eating day but with generous portions of medicine to counteract the effect of overeating on Christmas Day.

Originally this celebration dated back to the 4th century, after Christianity became the state religion of Rome. It consisted of wild drinking and sword dancing among other things. Later in about 1840, it took on the romantic and sentimental flavour which we know now. Christmas cards came in during the Victorian age. Nowadays more than a billion cards are sent all over the world.

It was in the mid-Victorian period that we began to offer people presents. Before that giving presents was a thing done at New Year. In Britain, we like to put up decorations at Christmas. Holly, ivy and mistletoe can be found everywhere. These plants were originally thought to be magical since they had berries when all other plants appeared to be dead. By the Twelfth Night after Christmas all decorations should have been removed, or the house in question will be hit by bad luck.

New Year's Day: Lots of people gather on this day in the squares of the cities. They all sing Auld Lang Syne and are mostly at least half-drunk. In northern England or Scotland there are some traditions that are linked to New Year. The Scots believe that if the first person to set foot in the house is tall and dark, he will bring good luck.

Easter: This celebrates the Resurrection of Christ from the dead. Most people try to get away for a three or four-day holiday to get a break from it all. And what about the famous Easter egg? This is big business for supporting the chocolate industry. Some more old fashioned families hide these eggs in the garden or in the house and leave the children to find them on Easter Sunday.

Guy Fawkes Day: This is a fiery celebration in Britain. On 5th November 1605 there was a plot to blow up the Houses of Parliament. The culprits were discovered and hanged. Since that time bonfires are made and lit on November 5th. Models of Guy Fawkes made of cloth are stuck in the middle of the bonfire and millions of fireworks are let off. Children go around in the week before collecting money with the words "Penny for the Guy". Nowadays this is all commercialised too. The author remembers times when friends and family used to bake potatoes and cheese on these bonfires. It was a great atmosphere.

LAUGHING A LITTLE

Have you seen the new aluminium Christmas trees?
You really can't tell them from the plastic ones.

You know what Christmas is like in the middle of a recession?
It's when your family looks on greedily as you carve the Big Mac.

20

PERFECT your PHRASALS

And here are the last ones – for now.

→ To tell the truth, Ernst enjoyed himself.

TELL

tell somebody's fortune	jemandem wahrsagen
tell stories	Märchen auftischen
tell a white lie	eine Notlüge gebrauchen
tell off	ausschimpfen
tell on	verraten

LAUGHING A LITTLE

Day Dreaming

René: Rob, if I were going to tell your fortune, I'd say you'd stay in Germany all your life.

Rob: No, not me. I've been planning to leave for a couple of years now. To tell the truth I'm sick of the place.

René: Don't tell stories, Rob. You've got a good job and lots of insurances. What more do you want.

Rob: I'd like to live in the sun. That's my ambition.

René: But then you wouldn't earn as much as you do at present.

Rob: Money isn't everything. Good climate and good food are just as important.

René: There you are, you see? You can stay in Germany and have everything – good salary, solarium and steak. What more do you want?

CULTURAL QUIZ for BRAINWARES

How do you deal with the following situations?

1. You get involved in a minor road accident with another car. It's heavy traffic. You both climb out. Your reaction is to
   a) become very angry as the other driver is at fault, you shout at him, traffic everywhere.
   b) get out of the car, you're not angry, you ask for his details, insurance policy, you leave quickly.
   c) Come to an amicable agreement, no need to take down details, you leave.

2. You are sitting in a peaceful park. A Brit sits next to you and nods to you. You feel like talking and ask him a few polite questions. He gives one-word answers. What's your reaction?
   a) to continue trying to make conversation even if he doesn't warm to it and only smiles
   b) to stop asking but still behave in a friendly way.
   c) to feel offended and leave. The Brits are cold and unfriendly.

3. You've been asked to go out for a meal with a colleague and his friends after work. It was just a casual invitation. You eat a good meal. At the end the friend/colleague takes out his money, his friends do the same. What is your reaction?
   a) you feel insulted since you were invited, hide it by insisting on paying the whole bill.
   b) you make no attempt to pay your share. You're embarrassed about going "Dutch" like this.
   c) you do as the others do, feeling no discomfort.

20

PLAYING with WORDS

Last but not least another little translation exercise.

Im indischen Restaurant

Jenny: Und heute morgen hatte ich eine Zigeunerin als Patientin, die mir aus der Hand lesen wollte.

Ernst: So, sie hat dir die Zukunft vorausgesagt, oder?

Jenny: Ja, sie sagte mir, dass ich Ende des Jahres verheiratet sein werde.

Ernst: Das muss eine Notlüge gewesen sein. Schließlich bist du ja noch mit mir zusammen.

Jenny: Ernst, ich wurde vor 27 Jahren geboren. Das bedeutet, es ist höchste Zeit, dass ich heirate.

Ernst: Natürlich, Jenny. Oje, ich bin vollkommen satt. Ich krieg keinen Bissen mehr runter.

Jenny: Ernst, ich glaube, du drückst dich vor dem Problem!

TIP of the day

Join events, see what they do. Don't compare with home! On special days book tables in advance. Keep smiling and you'll win.

CHAPTER 1

1. *At the back of his mind* is the English idiom.
2. *It came out of the blue* (meaning blue sky) is the English idiom.
3. "Handy" is translated as cell phone or mobile.

CHAPTER 2

1. Mein Schatz – sweetheart or darling in this meaning
2. Ernst is *serious*. There is a word *earnest* but this is rather old-fashioned.
3. Wenigstens – *at least*
4. Ehrlich gesagt – to be frank

CHAPTER 3

1. It's high time you + past tense ...
   It's high time you *learnt* this rule.
2. Lass es uns anpacken – *Let's take the bull by the horns* (idiom)
3. *Nonsense* here is much too strong, even rude. The natural answer is *of course not.*
4. Das hat mir gerade noch gefehlt – *Oh, that was all I needed*
5. Ein großes Maul und nichts dahinter – *you're all talk* (idiom)

CHAPTER 4

1. Information never takes an "s" in the end. This is the same for advice, progress, furniture, data ... (I need all the *information* I can get on that.)
2. Do, not make – to *do a course* in ...
3. Make, not do – to *make a mistake*
4. Ich habe Schwierigkeiten, das zu akzeptieren – I have a problem to accept that
5. Typisch für – typical *of*

CHAPTER 5

1. Es ist Zeit, dass wir gehen – *It's time we went* (see Chapter 3 Note 1)
2. Besser als – (here) *superior to*
3. Advice (always singular, see Chapter 4 note 1)
4. *Environmentally friendly* – environmentally is an adverb describing the adjective friendly.

5. Mehr als – *more than*
6. Was für ein tolles Wetter! – *What beautiful weather!* This is an idiomatic exclamation.

CHAPTER 6

1. Wir sind es gewohnt, ... zu bekommen – we are used *to* getting
   The "to" is not part of the verb, it is a preposition. After a preposition we have a gerund (-ing form).
2. Küche – *kitchen* (the room). The German refers to the kitchen equipment, and means it does not include kitchen furniture/equipment.
3. Heutzutage – *nowadays*
4. Schritte unternehmen – *take steps*
5. Ordnung muss sein – *you have to be properly organized*
6. Wir werden herumlaufen – in English we use the continuous form to emphasize that the action is continuing.
7. "What's about" is a mistake found in many books. Richtig: *What about ...* – wie wäre es mit/wie ist es mit ...?
8. Stadtwerke – *utilities company, electricity, gas company*
9. Auf Nummer sicher – to *be on the safe side*

CHAPTER 7

1. Warum das? Here: *What for?*
2. Ich würde ... gucken – I would be watching: Future continuous to emphasize that the action is continuing over a period.
3. Im Fernsehen – *on TV*
4. Das hast du in den falschen Hals bekommen – *you've got the wrong end of the stick* (idiom)
5. Ich nehme es – I'll take it. In German this future form is in fact a present, but not in English.
6. Scheiße! – literally "shit!" But we don't say it in English. It's primitive. We prefer *Oh, damn!*

CHAPTER 8

1. Nicht das Leichteste – *not as easy as he thought*
2. Er war gewohnt, etwas zu tun – *he was used to doing something. He was used to starting* work at ...
3. Wir reden aneinander vorbei – *we're talking at cross purposes*
4. nagelneu – *brand new*
5. Das ist absolut richtig. Ich bin nicht von hier. – *That's really true. I'm not from these parts.*
6. Wie peinlich! – *how embarrassing!*
7. So ein schlechtes Wetter! – *such bad weather* (idiomatic form)
8. Sie sind dünn wie eine Bohnenstange – *you are as thin as a rake* (idiom)

CHAPTER 9

1. Wir sind beide seit neun Uhr heute morgen bei der Arbeit – *We have both been at work since nine this morning.*
   since/for (seit) + present perfect
2. Ins Restaurant gehen – *to eat at a restaurant, to go to a restaurant*
3. Länger als – *longer than*
4. Sie sind alle eingepackt – *they are all in plastic packing*
5. In English we can't say: "a beef" – some roastbeef; swine is an old word for pork. A fish would be a complete fish swimming in the water.
6. Ich bin überrumpelt – *I am overwhelmed*
7. Reiß dich zusammen – *pull yourself together/pull your socks up!* (idiom)
8. Du isst kaum Fleisch – *you hardly eat meat*. Kaum – hardly, before the main verb.
9. Sensibel (dt.) – *sensitive* (engl.), it's a false friend; *sensible* (engl.) is vernünftig
10. Man lebt nur einmal – *You only live once*

CHAPTER 10

1. Sozusagen – *so to speak, as it were*
2. I'm not keen on + gerund (I'm not keen on eating meat)
3. nicht mein Fall – *not my cup of tea, not my thing*
4. Dieselbe Firma wie – *the same company as; same ... as*

5. With professions – Ich bin Lehrer – *I'm a teacher* – we use the indefinite article
6. Ich machte mein Studium – *I studied*
7. Auch das noch – *that's all I need*

CHAPTER 11

1. Ich sollte lieber was tun – *I ought to / should do something.*
2. Ich könnte sie zum Abendessen einladen – *I could invite her for dinner/ask her out for dinner*
3. Schritte unternehmen – to take steps
4. Do sport; get fit; we can also say *get ourselves fit*
5. Die meisten Leute – *most people*. We do not put "the" in front of it.
6. Die Sau rauslassen – *let one's hair down* (idiom)
7. Filme laufen im Kino – *films are shown at the cinema*

CHAPTER 12

1. Da muss er durch – *he must manage it* (idiom)
2. *Damages* – Schadenersatz; *damage* – Schaden/Schäden
3. In der Nähe – *nearby, in the vicinity*
4. *Eventuell* – perhaps; *eventually* – schließlich, am Ende
5. Es schmerzt/tut weh – *it hurts; pain* – der Schmerz
6. Mit anderen Worten – *in other words*
7. Sich blamieren – *make a fool of oneself; make oneself look stupid*
8. Diese Kleinigkeiten stören keinen großen Geist – *when the going gets tough the tough get going* (modern version/slogan)

CHAPTER 13

1. Keine Angst – *don't worry!* – es besteht keine Gefahr.
2. Straße – road or street. *Street* is used for Straßen in the town, not in the country (that would be a *road*).
3. Das Zimmer dreht sich. When we are drunk it is our heads that spin.
4. Im Moment – *at the minute/moment*
5. Es ist alles zu essen – *it's all to be eaten up*. Passive infinitive.
   Das Buch ist zu lesen – *the book is to be read.*
6. Konkurrenz – *competition*; Konkurrent – *competitor*

7. Another false friend: rentabel (dt.) – *viable, profitable; rentable* (engl.) – mietbar
8. Das gehört zur Kultur – *that's part of the culture* (German idiomatic form)

CHAPTER 14

1. Ich habe Impulse genug – *I have enough impulses.* "Enough" stands in front of the noun.
2. Natürlich – *of course.* In this meaning it's an adverb.
3. Ich wollte sagen – *I was trying to say*
4. *We've been broken into.* Present perfect, action finished and we can still see the result of it.
5. Ich sage Ihnen, wie – *I'll tell you how*
6. Das ist ein Land der Diebe – *this country is full of thieves*
7. Das ist euer England – *that's England for you* (idiomatic form)
8. Verdorben – *spoilt* (of children); verdorbene Gesellschaft – *corrupt* society

CHAPTER 15

1. Die Zeit vergeht wie im Flug – *how time flies* (saying)
2. Ich bin seit Dezember hier – *I have been her since December.* Present perfect with "since".
3. Jemand hat ihn denunziert – *somebody had blown the whistle on him*
4. Schuld – *guilt* (vor Gericht); Schuld – *fault* (Charakter; Fehler)
5. Übernehmen – *to take over; to overtake* – (Auto) überholen
6. Zusammenbrechen – *collapse.* The building collapsed during the earthquake.
7. Was für ein Glück! – *What luck!* As an exclamation.
8. Absolutely describes the adjective "unexpected". Therefore it is an adverb (with -ly).

CHAPTER 16

1. Genie – *genius; genie* (engl.) – böser Geist
2. *Als* ich ... war – *when* I was ...
3. Konkurrenz – *competition; concurrence* (engl.) – Übereinstimmung (another false friend)
4. Im Fernsehen – *on television*
5. Meiner Meinung nach – *in my opinion; meaning* – Bedeutung (yet another false friend)
6. *Auf* der anderen Seite – *on the other hand*
7. Wenn schon, denn schon – *in for a penny, in for a pound* (English proverb)
8. Blau – *drunk, merry. Blue* rather means depressed (singing the blues).
9. Jemanden erwarten – *expect somebody*

CHAPTER 17

1. Alles im Griff – *everything's under control*
2. Eine Diät machen – *be on a diet*
3. Nicht lebenswert sein – *it's not worth living*. After "it's not worth" we must use the gerund (-ing from).
4. Ich arbeite viel – *I work hard; hardly* means kaum
5. Ich gönne mir ja sonst nichts – *I've no other pleasure in life* (German idiom)
6. zunehmen – *to put on weight*
7. Wie lange/seit wann existiert es? – *How long has it existed?*
8. Wir sollten nicht übertreiben – *we shouldn't exaggerate*

CHAPTER 18

1. Nachrichten – *news*. "News" is singular in English: The news is ...
2. Politik – *politics*; it's a plural form but: politics is ...
3. Wir nennen es – *we call it*
4. (Müll-)Verbrennungsanlage – *incineration plant*
5. Es wird furchtbar stinken – *it'll smell terrible*
6. Während eines Meetings – *during* a meeting. Problems occur because "während" is "during" and "while".

7. So schnell, wie es geht – *as quickly/as fast as possible*
8. 'Avoid' is followed by a gerund – *avoid allowing*
9. Däumchen drehen – *to twiddle one's thumbs* (idiom)

CHAPTER 19

1. Keinen blassen Schimmer haben – *I haven't got the least idea* (idiomatic form)
2. Viel von meiner Zeit – *a lot of my time*. In positive sentences it's better to use "a lot of", with negatives and questions "much".
3. Bitte schön – *there you are*. Use this form when passing or giving something to somebody.
4. Alle fünf Minuten – *every five minutes*
5. Unabhängig davon – *apart from that*; unabhängig is *independent* as an adjective
6. England ist nicht das Schlechteste/Es gibt Schlimmeres als das – *There are worse places than England*
7. Oder? (as a question tag) – (here) *can we?* You must use question tags and not forms such as "or?", "nehh?", "wa?".
8. Entschuldigung/was/wie bitte? – *excuse me, what did you say?* "Apology" means eine Entschuldigung.

CHAPTER 20

1. *Sympathisch* – friendly, nice; *sympathetic* – voll Mitgefühl (another false friend)
2. Heiliger Abend/Heiligabend – *Christmas Eve*
3. Ich bin geboren – *I was born.* 'I am born' does not exist.
4. Alle sollten lieber – *everybody should/ought to*. German form is idiomatic.
5. Ist was? Was ist los? – *Is anything wrong?/What's wrong?*
6. Ein fauler Hund – *a lazybones*
7. Wie es sich gehört – *as one should* (idiomatic German).
8. To express being full of food – I'm full, I'm bloated, I'm stuffed full
9. *Bis bald – see you later/see you soon*

CHAPTER 1

Laughing at grammar

a) was asked / replied
b) do you farm / have you lived
c) was charged / acquitted / went / to get / won / want

Cultural quiz for brainwares

1. a) Edinburgh b) Cardiff c) Belfast
2. c) Liverpool
3. Wales
4. Scotland / the kilt
5. The Queen Mother
6. Western Ireland, Western Scotland, Northern Wales, Brittany in France
7. Battle of Hastings, 1066
8. Cornwall, Devon, Somerset
9. Pennines
10. Cider

Playing with words

1. Ernst came home late and looked rather miserable. "What have you been getting up to?" Jenny wanted to know.
2. Since Ernst got his new job, he has been getting too big for his boots.
3. The policeman stopped Ernst for driving too fast, but because he's a foreigner he got away with it.
4. Jenny and Ernst weren't earning enough so they got into hot water with their bank regarding their mortgage.

CHAPTER 2

Laughing at grammar

a) asked / knew / was / do you weigh / said
b) do you have / haven't shaken
c) have / do / take

Cultural quiz for brainwares

1. British Telecom
2. Sun (B) / Guardian (H) / Observer (H) / Times (H) / Daily Express (B) / Mirror (B) / Telegraph (H), Evening Standard (H)
3. b) five (BBC 1, BBC 2, ITV, Channel 4, Channel 5)
4. Football
5. Rugby
6. a) golf-course / b) pitch / c) court / d) track
7. DM 3,20 = £ 1
8. Stonehenge
9. The British flag
10. In towns = b) 30 mph / outside towns = a) 60 mph

Playing with words

1. up to 2. fish out of water 3. kicked out

CHAPTER 3

Laughing at grammar

a) did you hear / phoned / we are checking / we have noticed / answered / I don't have / did not

b) was giving / asked / I am / call up / tell / you tell him / he is shaving

c) told / was

Cultural quiz for brainwares

1. Gatwick, Heathrow, Stansted, City of London
2. Margaret Thatcher
3. It's the typical English bus with an upstairs and a downstairs.
4. Fish and chips
5. Curry
6. Indian, Chinese
7. Scones, a sort of sweet bread or cake, strawberry or raspberry jam, double cream
8. Cheese
9. Bed and Breakfast
10. We raise our glasses and wish them success and health.

Playing with words

Ernst: Okay, let's get on with it. We have to talk about my trip to England, haven't we?

Mother: I think it will do you good. It's high time you stood on your own feet. You're always talking about travelling, but you never do anything about it.

Ernst: That's just what I needed. Thanks for your support. Do you want to pick a quarrel with me? I've come to ask your advice.

Mother: Of course, my dear boy. Be careful! You're driving too quickly. You are in a built-up area.

1. of course not
2. representative
3. fetch
4. are picking holes in me

CHAPTER 4

Laughing at grammar

a) boring / to challenge / went / beating / was dribbling / lumbering / killing / killing / to kill / to trip

b) to change / change

Cultural quiz for brainwares

1. Loch Ness
2. Windermere, Derwent Water, Bassenthwaite Lake, Crummock Water, Thirlmere Lake
3. Fawlty Towers, Monty Python's Flying Circus
4. Pink Panther
5. Churchill
6. Lancashire against Yorkshire
7. Six / he had two beheaded, he divorced two, one died and one survived him (divorced, beheaded, died, divorced, beheaded, survived)
8. the Conservative Party
9. 1666
10. The state radio broadcasting company – British Broadcasting Corporation.

Playing with words

a) 1. pack up 2. made 3. of

b) Mother: Ernst, don't raise your voice to me.
Ernst: Come on, let's pack in arguing. It's not worth it.
Mother: You are only going to England because of this girl and not for the work. You can believe me. She'll pack you off when you start boring her. And you'll have to manage by yourself.
Ernst: Thank you very much for your support.

CHAPTER 5

Laughing at grammar

a) walked / are / was / be / was
b) being
c) be
d) was broken / decorated

Cultural quiz for brainwares

1. b) terraced
2. c) estate agent
3. Green fingers
4. Do it yourself
5. Three meters / 1 m = 1.0936 yards = 39.37 inches = 2.87 feet
6. 1.43 pints in one litre
7. By the number of rooms
8. Scones, toast, jam and a lot of tea at 4 p.m.
9. Pork sausages, fried bread, eggs, bacon, fried tomatoes and baked beans
10. c) owned houses

Playing with words

1. thinks highly
2. thinks twice
3. some advice
4. where is the cottage located / built / renovated

CHAPTER 6

Laughing at grammar

a) seeing, hearing or meeting b) keeping c) knowing

Cultural quiz for brainwares

1. b) Terraced house
2. c) Bed and Breakfast
3. They go to an estate agent where a picture of the house or flat is displayed in the window. In addition estate agents put a big sign in front of the house saying "To Sell".
4. a) Hull
5. Queen Victoria
6. They are the two furthest ends of Britain (north of Scotland, south west of England).
7. In Scotland
8. Two upstairs, two downstairs (possibly three upstairs)
9. Snowdon, Ben Nevis, Ben Nevis
10. This is a wall built to protect the Romans from the Scots. It stretches across northern England.

Playing with words

Ernst: Hi Jenny, *what about going* to a disco this evening? I feel a bit lively.

Jenny: Oh, I don't know. I am on early shift tomorrow at the hospital.

Ernst: *Don't worry! To be an the safe side we* can leave at eleven so we'll back to the cottage early.

Jenny: And then you'll want to go to the Indian takeaway. We'll be back after midnight.

Ernst: *I know, I'm used to eating late*, but tonight I promise you, no late night snacks even though *it's difficult to break a habit.*

CHAPTER 7

Laughing at grammar

a) had
b) are not
c) I die
d) dropped
e) write
f) become / become
g) was / didn't need
h) would be
i) are
j) don't mind

Cultural quiz for brainwares

1. b) furniture
2. a) going, going, gone
3. c) oak
4. It's a large piece of furniture for keeping books or plates in. It has two doors at the front.
5. a) booty b) beams
6. Antique
7. Boot fair, auction, jumble sale
8. Bid
9. a) under the house b) under the roof c) at the back of a car
10. Union Jack

Playing with words

a) Jenny: Jesus, I'm completely tired out. I've had a lousy day at work.
Ernst: I can see that. *You look a sight.* What on earth happened? Did you have to *look after* a difficult patient?
Jenny: That was part of it. And then there was a power failure twice. That didn't help matters.
Ernst: Yes, I heard something about that *on the TV.* (The doorbell rings.) *Oh, my goodness.* That's the door. *I'll get it*. It's somebody from the hospital for you.
Jenny: Oh, not again!

b) 1. put something in it
2. put it in a safe place
3. make a room out of it
4. put my writing things in it
5. cook it at Christmas
(these answers are subjective)

CHAPTER 8

Laughing at grammar

a) shouldn't you? / haven't I? / didn't you? / doesn't it? / does it?
b) isn't it? / have you? / hadn't I?
c) can you?
d) didn't you? / did she?

Cultural quiz for brainwares

1. Germany = 44.9 Italy = 42.4 Britain = 42
2. to go to the toilet
3. pass on / pass over / go
4. How are you?
5. a) A special sort of raincoat
   b) Scottish cloth with special chequered patterns on it
   c) A suit patterned with thin lines worn by businessmen in London
   d) Punch is a satirical magazine.
   e) Earl Grey is a type of tea with a special unmistakable flavour.

Playing with words

Boss: And you've been here for almost six months now. What are your feelings about things?

Ernst: *It wasn't as easy as I thought – I had to take over* a lot of extra responsibility. But I've got it together now.

Boss: I heard some members of staff were painting all sorts of black pictures for you.

Ernst: That's right. But as you told me at the beginning *I have to take it with a pinch of salt or I would take to drink / start drinking.* That's not happened. How *embarrassing* that would have been.

Boss: I hope not. Well, I see you're settling in better now.

Ernst: Without any doubt! And now *I've even got used to working* these unusual hours, I mean nine to five with the occasional Saturday.

Boss: Good, because if you get promoted, the hours will become even more unusual, as you put it.

CHAPTER 9

Laughing at grammar

a) at | b) from … to
c) on / in | d) next to / above / with / above/over / on

Cultural quiz for brainwares

1. b) Indian
2. a) putting articles in and pushing it around
   b) putting on top of all the floorboards to cover them up
   c) changing into sports clothes before playing a sport
3. a) hypermarket
4. corner shop
5. a) 48 million
6. a) German
7. c) the continent
8. c) you're o.k., you're a fair bloke, thumbs up
9. Beer and spirits
10. b) Tesco

Playing with words

Ernst: *I've been looking for somebody* to help me for five minutes. It's terrible.

Assistant: Sorry, sir. We're very busy. How can I help you?

Ernst: Well look, *all these lamb chops are packed up / pre-packed*. I'd like to have them separately.

Assistant: Sorry, sir. They are all in vacuum packaging and individually selected.

Ernst: Well, *I fancy/feel like going somewhere* else. It's all so mechanised, *so impersonal. I don't feel at ease* without the personal touch.

Assistant: I suggest you go elsewhere then, sir.

CHAPTER 10

Laughing at grammar

a) of / by
b) with / opposite / at / of / between / with / to
c) on / on / up
d) behind / for

Cultural quiz for brainwares

1. b) your Christian name
2. c) let's tackle
3. b) that's all I need
4. Aus einem Kieselstein kann man keinen Diamanten schleifen.
5. a) nervous
   b) certain
   c) board
   d) succeed
6. b) coming to the party uninvited
7. Gin / Geneva / Dutch gin
8. b) out of a newspaper
9. c) crisps
10. c) overeating and drinking

Playing with words

1. I had *a lot to* drink at the party last night and this morning I had some pressure in my head, *as it were / so to speak.*
2. Ernst: Well, I can tell you honestly, these parties are *not my cup of tea.*
3. Boss: I heard you were out drinking pretty hard with some members of staff last night.
   Ernst: No, not really, well yes. Actually *you've got the wrong end of the stick.*
4. Ernst: You really don't like Viv very much, *do you?*
   Jill: Well, since you mention it, no!
   Ernst: I know. She needs *taking down a peg or two.*
5. Ernst: Where've you been? I was *expecting* you at 7 p.m.
   Jenny: Well, to tell the truth, England is getting so violent.
   Ernst: I know, and you're thinking of *taking up* Karate or self-defence.
   Jenny: You've hit the nail on the head!

CHAPTER 11

Laughing at grammar

a) believes
b) he's always opening / am
c) I've been looking
d) love / love / has been / are calling / are talking / do you think
e) separates / prints
f) sounds / has

Cultural quiz for brainwares

1. Five
2. b) Beatrix Potter
3. The Tube
4. a) Guardian (all the others are boulevard press)
5. The Open University
6. b) West End
7. Lord of the Rings (Tolkien)
8. Manchester United
9. Vegetarian
10. Mr Bean

Playing with words

1. b) let his hair down
2. does his best
3. do away with
4. doing it up
5. a) commute   b) musical   c) audience

CHAPTER 12

Laughing at grammar

a) in / over by / in b) to / out c) on d) after / before

Cultural quiz for brainwares

1. National Health Service
2. c) 3 million
3. A referral
4. a) prescription
5. Illness, disease
6. a) pull it out
7. a) crown
8. A wall built across the country between Scotland and England. It was built by the Romans to keep the Scots out.
9. b) fourth finger, left hand
10. b) Once upon a time there was ...

Playing with words

1. Doctor: Now where exactly does it hurt, Mr Lachnit?
   Ernst: *Well, it hurts me* in the area of my stomach.
   Doctor: Where about? Here?
   Ernst: Ouch! Yes there! It's *near to my ribs.*
   Doctor: When did the trouble start? When did you first notice it?
   Ernst: Yesterday morning. After my jog. Doctor, doctor, I'm sure it's my liver. I'm going to die.
   Doctor: Mr Lachnit, you're reacting too quickly.
   Ernst: *I'm sure I have some damage in my body.* Liver, heart, gall bladder. *Somehow every time I do sport I make a fool of myself.* I get injured.

2. a) rounds b) self-medication
   c) insure yourself d) pamper

CHAPTER 13

Laughing at grammar

a) had fixed b) wanted / cost
c) never had to get ... d) had launched / won / would get

Cultural quiz for brainwares

1. a) Britain, because the government has put a very high tax on it
2. Old age pensioner
3. a) A motorway, normally three lanes
   b) A secondary road, like a dual carriageway
4. It's the safety lane at the side of the motorway that cars can run onto in an emergency.
5. There are two of them – the A. A. (Automobile Association) and the R.A.C. (Royal Automobile Club)
6. He's buying a loaf of bread.
7. A fried egg
8. She has impressed her style, methods and attitudes on Britain so that we can see her influence in it.
9. Queen Elizabeth, the Queen Mother, Charles, Edward, Andrew, William, Anne, Philip, etc.
10. Darts

Playing with words

1. Ernst: It's really great to be camping over here in this camping bus. *At the moment* I feel really relaxed.

Jenny: Yes, but I'm afraid there's no electricity on this campsite.

Ernst: *Don't worry!* We won't actually need it for a couple of days. We can use the gas that's *left over.*

Jenny: Well, we'll certainly have some peace and quiet here. There's no soul around.

Ernst: Yes, I'm sure we'll be *left in peace* here. That's good after all the noise of the city. And *some hardship is a part of the sport* of camping.

Jenny: To tell the truth there's not much hardship in living in this luxury camper.

CHAPTER 14

Laughing at grammar

a) loved
b) was / was / could / had been / had just happened / would / tasted / could
c) had been / had been

Cultural quiz for brainwares

1. A wig
2. 12
3. A uniformed policeman
4. Beat
5. Guilty
6. A truncheon (Knüppel)
7. a) sentenced
8. c) sent down
9. The Queen
10. The Criminal Court in London

Playing with words

Sergeant: So, if you could just describe to me what happened, Mr Lachnit.

Ernst: Yes, sir. I was just coming out of my office when I saw that somebody was trying to *break into* the off-licence on the other side of the road.

Sergeant: What did this individual look like? Can you remember?

Ernst: *Of course! He was very tall and well-built. He weighed* about one hundred kilos. He ran out with the money and *broke into* a car at the side of the road. *But don't worry,* I got the car's number.

CHAPTER 15

Laughing at grammar

a) to / out / into
b) to / up through / towards / of / down / to / to / by / at

Cultural quiz for brainwares

1. Managing Director / CEO = Chief Executive Office
2. Promotion
3. To tell tales or stories to denounce Ernst
4. The boss at the top makes decisions and gives orders to be passed down to the lower levels.
5. The trade union
6. Queuing
7. If two people or more go out to the pub each one pays for himself.
8. a) divorce b) life/birth
   c) youth d) House of Commons

Playing with words

a) how time flies b) fault c) appointed
d) out e) can f) on with

CHAPTER 16

Laughing at grammar

a) had known b) what is the point c) worked
d) would never have been e) know

Cultural quiz for brainwares

1. Skegness
2. Smog
3. Big Brother
4. It's the Queen's official residence
5. The Lake District
6. Coronation Street / Eastenders
7. A spot
8. Golf
9. Cricket
10. A British sports car

Playing with words

Ladies and Gentlemen,
I'd like to thank you for coming today. I'll come to the point directly. Our competitors are very active. In my opinion we have to defend ourselves against this. I reckon that means we have to start a television campaign. We'll reach a lot of people. In the other hand this sort of advertising is very expensive. Anyway, I'm sure that something will come of this project.

CHAPTER 17

Laughing at grammar

a) up / down b) at c) out
d) out of e) after / out f) with / after / in

Cultural quiz for brainwares

1. Approximately 60.3 kilos
2. The NHS (National Health Service)
3. Register
4. Self-medication
5. b) public school c) private school
6. b) boarding school
7. 'A' Level
8. The Archbishop of Canterbury
9. Irish Sea, North Sea, English Channel
10. Aran

Playing with words

Ernst: Jenny, I know *you were complaining* about my weight. Anyhow, *I've been on a diet* in the last three weeks.
Jenny: Well, what was the result of that?
Ernst: You won't believe it but *I've lost two kilos. I'm getting as thin as a rake.*
Jenny: Yes, you look better. How did you do it?
Ernst: Well, *I avoided all* all sorts of fried food, beer and grease. And I've taken up jogging and swimming again.
Jenny: Go for it, Ernst!

CHAPTER 18

Laughing at grammar

a) were / let / you would (you'd) get up b) were / would get
c) wears

Cultural quiz for brainwares

1. BBC World Service
2. Big Ben
3. The Cheviots
4. They are islands off the northern tip of Scotland
5. He dresses up in a uniform, stands in front of the town hall and reads the important news to the people.
6. Monopoly
7. Westminster Abbey
8. St. Paul's Cathedral
9. The Tower of London
10. The Beefeaters

Playing with words

1. Ernst: Hmmm. *Something smells good* here. What is it?
   Waiter: That's the venison pie, sir.
   Ernst: Well, *I'll certainly have that.* And could I have a bottle of red wine *during the meal*, with the main course?
   Waiter: Certainly, sir.
   Ernst: Well, Jenny, *things are better for us since* I got my promotion. We *call that* really good luck!

2. a) a petition b) to commission c) minority

CHAPTER 19

Laughing at grammar

a) do you want / to find / had lost / had / picked / was
b) had just set up / heard / picked / discuss / said

Cultural quiz for brainwares

1. valid insurance / Ministry of Transport Certificate (TÜV), current driving licence
2. A stick the police use to beat criminals
3. Driving licence
4. Number plate
5. There isn't one.
6. b) a man who buys and sells houses
7. a) tax advisor
8. c) defence council

Playing with words

Policeman: (waving at Ernst) Could you *pull over*, please? Now then, sir. What do you think you're doing?
Ernst: I haven't the *the faintest idea* what you're talking about. What have I done wrong?
Policeman: You're driving the wrong way down a one-way street.
Ernst: *You're pulling my leg*. I didn't see a sign. I'm not from these parts, you know.
Policeman: *You'd better pull yourself together* or there'll be problems.
Ernst: Hmmm. England's not the worst.

CHAPTER 20

Laughing at grammar

a) at / with
b) by (from) / of
c) on / from / of
d) older / the louder
e) eating / drinking / watching
f) won't you
g) think / would be / got

Cultural quiz for brainwares

1. b) It's always more sensible to get details and report the matter to the police. Causing a big argument is primitive and will cause more problems. Generally, British drivers are polite and do not toot their horns or do the "Lichthupe".
2. b) Many Brits are reserved and keep themselves to themselves. Don't force yourself onto the person. If he gives you a friendly nod it still doesn't mean that he wants to talk to you.
3. c) If you are a special guest your host may pay. Otherwise everybody goes "Dutch". There's no reason to feel uncomfortable with this.

Playing with words

At the Indian restaurant

Jenny: And this morning I had a gipsy patient who wanted to read my hands.
Ernst: So she told your fortune, did she?
Jenny: Yes, she told me I could be married by the end of the year.
Ernst: That must have been a white lie. After all you're still going out with me.
Jenny: Ernst, I was born twenty-seven years ago. That means it's high time I was married.
Ernst: Of course, Jenny. Oh dear, I'm completely full. I can't eat another thing.
Jenny: Ernst, I think you're avoiding the problem!

abilities	*Fähigkeiten*
absurdity	*Absurdität*
accommodation	*Unterbringung*
accompany	*begleiten*
accuse	*anklagen, vorwerfen*
accustomed to	*gewohnt sein zu*
acquaintance	*Bekanntschaft*
acquit	*freisprechen*
ad(vertisement)	*(Zeitungs-)Anzeige*
adamant	*hart, unerbittlich*
adapt	*anpassen*
admire	*bewundern*
admit	*zugeben*
advance	*Fortschritt, Weiterkommen*
adventurous	*abenteuerlich*
advice	*Hinweis, Ratschlag*
aid	*helfen*
ailment	*Leiden*
albeit	*trotz(dem)*
ale	*Bier*
aloof	*distanziert, reserviert*
amazing	*erstaunlich*
amenities	*Annehmlichkeiten*
amiable	*freundschaftlich*
anglicise	*anglisieren, "englisch" werden*
annoy	*verärgern*
ant	*Ameise*
applicant	*Bewerber*
appointment	*(Arzt-)Termin*
approach	*annähern, Annäherung*
art	*Kunst*
assault	*Überfälle*
attempt	*Versuch*
attention	*Aufmerksamkeit*
attic	*Boden, Speicher (unter dem Dach)*
attitude	*Ansicht, Meinung, Einstellung*

auction	*Auktion*
auctioneer	*Auktionator*
audience	*Zuschauer, Zuhörer*
authorities	*Behörden, Vorgesetzte*
available	*zur Verfügung stehen, vorhanden*
average	*Durchschnitt*
bang	*knallen*
bank account	*Bankkonto*
bank clerk	*Bankangestellter*
bank statement	*Kontoauszug*
banner	*Fahne, Banner*
bargain	*günstiges Geschäft, Schnäppchen*
barrel	*Fass*
bat an eyelid	*mit der Wimper zucken*
bath tub	*Badewanne*
battery hen	*Legehenne*
be at fault	*Fehler gemacht haben*
beetle	*Käfer*
behave	*verhalten, benehmen*
behest	*Geheiß, Befehl*
belongings	*Habseligkeiten, Sachen*
bid	*bieten (Auktion)*
bidder	*Bieter*
bill	*Rechnung*
biting	*gemein, boshaft*
bloke	*Typ, Kerl*
board a train	*einen Zug besteigen, einsteigen*
boarding school	*Internat*
boastful	*angeberisch*
Bobby	*engl. uniformierter Polizist*
boil	*kochen*
bonfire	*Lagerfeuer*
boom	*dröhnen*
boot	*Kofferraum des Autos*
booty	*Beute*
bore	*langweilen*

borrow	*ausleihen, borgen*
bossy	*bestimmend, herrisch*
bother	*nerven, ärgern*
bottom line	*Tenor, Grundidee*
boundaries	*Grenzen*
bowels	*Verdauungsorgane, Darm*
brain	*Gehirn*
branch	*Zweigstelle, Niederlassung*
break	*Durchbruch, Pause*
breed	*Zucht, Spezies*
bride	*Braut*
broadcast	*Sender*
browse	*durchstöbern*
buck a system	*das System unterlaufen*
building society	*Baugesellschaft*
bump	*knallen, rempeln, zufällig treffen*
burden	*Last*
bureau	*Schreibtisch*
bury	*begraben, eingraben*
busker	*Straßenmusikant*
bustle	*geschäftig hin und her eilen*
button	*Knopf*
calories	*Kalorien*
campaign	*Kampagne*
camper	*Wohnmobil*
cantankerous	*streitlustig*
capture	*retten, mitnehmen*
carbohydrates	*Kohlenhydrate*
carpet	*Teppich*
cart away	*in einem Karren/Wagen davonschaffen*
cartilage	*Meniskus*
cartwheel	*Schippkarre*
carve	*schaben*
casually	*zwanglos*
catch	*Haken, Nachteil*
cater for	*beliefern, besorgen*

celebrate	*feiern*
cellar	*Keller*
cellular, cell phone	*Handy*
chairman	*Vorsitzender*
challenge	*herausfordern*
chap	*Typ, Kerl*
charge	*anklagen; vorwerfen*
charity	*Wohltätigkeit*
charmer	*Charmeur*
charming	*schön, ansprechend*
chatter	*klönen, ungezwungen sprechen, schnattern*
cheer	*applaudieren, zustimmen*
chime	*dröhnen, klingen,*
chimney	*Schornstein*
chip in	*(ins Gespräch) einmischen*
choice	*(Aus-)Wahl*
civil servant	*Beamter*
claim form	*Zeugenbefragungsbogen*
cling to	*festhalten an*
clink	*klicken*
clue	*Hinweis, Idee, Ahnung*
clutch	*an sich drücken*
collide	*kollidieren, zusammenstoßen*
colloquial	*umgangssprachlich*
come up roses	*alles war rosig*
commission	*beauftragen*
commuter	*Pendler*
compare	*vergleichen*
competition	*Wettbewerb*
competitor	*Mitbewerber, Konkurrent*
complain	*beschweren, jammern*
concern	*betreffen*
conclusion	*Ergebnis, Schluss, Entscheidung*
conduct	*Verhalten(sweise)*
confuse	*durcheinander bringen*

consist of	*bestehen aus*
console	*trösten*
constable	*Polizist*
constitution	*Verfassung*
consult a doctor	*einen Arzt konsultieren*
consume	*konsumieren*
contentment	*Zufriedenheit*
contest	*Wettbewerb*
contract	*Vertrag*
contradictions	*Widersprüche*
convenience	*Bequemlichkeit*
convert	*umwandeln, verwandeln*
convict	*verurteilen*
convince	*überzeugen*
cope with	*fertig werden mit*
cosy	*gemütlich*
council	*hier: die Stadt*
counteract	*entgegenwirken*
county	*Grafschaft, Region*
crackle away	*vor sich hin knistern und knattern*
crash down	*abstürzen, herunterstürzen*
creak	*knarren und quietschen*
create	*erzeugen*
creep	*kriechen*
crewed	*besetzt, bemannt sein mit*
crime	*Verbrechen*
crime rate	*Verbrechensrate*
crisis	*Krise, Problem*
cross	*verärgert*
cruelty	*Grausamkeit*
culprit	*Schuldiger*
cure	*Kur, Medizin, Heilung*
custard	*Vanillecreme*
cutlet	*Kotelett*
damp	*Feuchtigkeit*
dangerous	*gefährlich*

dare	*wagen*
decision	*Entscheidung*
decorate	*tapezieren und streichen*
deed	*Tat*
degenerated	*heruntergekommen, verfallen*
delete	*löschen*
delicious	*lecker, gut schmeckend*
delightful	*entzückend, erfreulich*
demand	*Nachfrage*
denounce	*verurteilen, denunzieren*
dependent on	*abhängig von*
depressing	*deprimierend, bedrückend*
descent	*(hier:) Abstammung*
destination	*Ziel, Bestimmungsort*
detached house	*Einzelhaus*
differ	*unterscheiden, verschieden sein*
digestion	*Verdauung*
direct debit	*Einzugsermächtigung*
disadvantage	*Nachteil*
disappoint	*enttäuschen*
discomfort	*Unbequemlichkeit*
disease	*Krankheit*
disentangle	*sich losreißen, befreien von*
dislike	*nicht mögen, unsympathisch finden*
disrespectful	*respektlos, unfreundlich*
divisive	*trennen, unterscheiden (nach sozialen Kriterien)*
divorce rate	*Scheidungsrate*
do a degree	*Diplom machen*
do one's rounds	*Visite machen*
do overtime	*Überstunden machen*
documentary	*Dokumentarfilm*
dollop	*Nachschlag, Portionen*
donation	*Spende*
dour	*mürrisch*
draught	*Zug*

dressing	*(Salat-)Dressing, Sauce*
dribble	*dribbeln*
drumstick	*Hühnerkeule, Trommelstock*
due care	*gebührende Sorgfalt*
dust	*Staub*
economical	*sparsam*
edge	*Rand, Ecke*
effort	*Anstrengung, Bemühung*
emerge	*auftauchen*
emphasis	*Betonung, Schwerpunkt*
emphasize	*betonen, hervorheben*
encounter	*begegnen*
enlightenment	*Aufklärung*
entertainment	*Unterhaltung*
entrust	*anvertrauen*
environment	*Umgebung, Umwelt*
equivalent	*Entsprechung*
error	*Fehler*
essentials	*das Notwendigste*
estate agent	*Immobilienmakler*
event	*Ereignis*
eventually	*letztendlich, am Ende*
evict	*rausschmeißen, vertreiben*
exaggerate	*übertreiben*
excess baggage	*zusätzliches Gepäck*
exchange rate	*Umrechnungskurs*
excitement	*Aufregung*
excursion	*Exkursion, Ausflug*
executive	*Führungskraft*
exhaustion	*Erschöpfung*
expenses	*Ausgaben*
expire	*auslaufen, fällig werden*
expression	*Ausdruck*
faithful	*treu*
famous/infamous	*berühmt/berüchtigt*
fancy	*bevorzugen, Lust drauf haben*

farce	*Farce*
fat	*fett, dick*
fatigue	*Ermüdung, Schwäche*
fellow	*Typ, Kerl*
fellow-workers	*Kollegen*
festive day	*Feiertag*
fiddle	*rumfummeln*
fiery	*feurig*
filing	*Ablage*
fine	*Strafgeld, Strafe*
fit	*fit, gesund*
flabby	*schlaff*
flat	*Wohnung*
flavour	*Geschmack(srichtung)*
float	*(an der Oberfläche) schwimmen*
flock	*zusammenkommen, eine Herde bilden*
fool	*Narr, Idiot*
fool round	*Blödsinn/Quatsch machen*
force	*Kraft, Macht*
former	*früher, ehemalig*
fortnight	*14 Tage, zwei Wochen*
fortress	*Fort, Burg*
forwarding address	*Nachsendeadresse*
frankly	*offen und ehrlich*
freight car	*Lieferwagen*
furious	*verärgert, böse*
furnished	*möbliert*
garrulous	*geschwätzig, redselig*
gather	*ver-/ansammeln*
gaze	*starren*
generalisation	*Verallgemeinerung*
generous	*freigiebig*
genre	*Genre*
gesture	*Geste*
get at	*anspielen, hinauswollen*
get the "hots" for somebody	*auf jemanden "scharf" sein*

glitter	*glänzen, schimmern*
go for a song	*für 'nen Apfel und 'n Ei weggehen*
grab	*greifen, zupacken*
gradually	*langsam, Stück für Stück*
grate	*Gitter, Rost*
gravy	*dunkle Bratensauce*
greed	*Geiz*
greenery	*Grünlandschaften*
grin	*grinsen*
grind to a halt	*zum Stillstand bringen*
groom	*Bräutigam*
grunt	*grunzen*
guardian	*Wächter*
habit	*Angewohnheit*
haggis	*Haggis (Innereien vom Schaf, im Schafsmagen gekocht); schottisches Gericht*
halve s.th.	*etwas halbieren*
handle	*(Slang, hier:) Name*
hangover	*Kater (vom Alkohol)*
hard shoulder	*Standspur*
hardened criminal	*verstockter, uneinsichtiger Verbrecher*
hardship	*Leiden*
hardy	*zäh, robust*
have none of it	*nicht mit sich reden lassen*
heartburn	*Sodbrennen*
hero	*Held*
hesitation	*Zögern*
high-brow	*Intellektuelle(r)*
hinder	*behindern, verhindern*
hint	*Hinweis, Tipp*
hiss	*zischen*
hob	*Kamin, Ofen*
holly	*Stechpalme*
hopeful	*hoffnungsvoll*
horseradish	*Meerrettich*
horticultural	*gartenbaulich*

host	*Gastgeber*
hovel	*(Vieh-)Schuppen*
huge	*hoch, viel, extrem*
humble	*bescheiden*
ignore	*ignorieren*
imagination	*Vorstellungsvermögen*
imbibe	*trinken, in sich aufnehmen*
immediately	*sofort, direkt*
immigration	*Immigration, Einwanderung*
impart	*überbringen*
impatient	*ungeduldig*
impress, impressed	*beeindrucken, beeindruckt*
impression	*Eindruck*
incineration plant, incinerator	*(Müll-)Verbrennungsanlage*
income tax	*Einkommensteuer*
indefinitely	*unendlich*
indigestion	*Verdauungsprobleme*
indiscriminately	*ohne Unterschiede zu machen*
indulge in	*sich hingeben, frönen*
industrious	*arbeitsam*
inebriated	*benebelt*
inevitable	*unvermeidlich*
inhabitant	*Einwohner*
initiate	*verursachen, ins Leben rufen*
injure	*verletzen*
in-laws	*Schwiegereltern*
insist on	*bestehen auf*
instructions	*Anweisung, Anleitung*
insult	*beleidigen*
insurance policy	*Versicherungspolice*
insure	*versichern*
intake	*Aufnahme*
intend	*beabsichtigen*
interval	*Intervall, Pause*
investigate	*herausfinden, erforschen*
issue	*Thema*

it's no good crying over spilt milk	*was passiert ist, ist passiert*
ivy	*Efeu*
jail	*Gefängnis*
jumble sale	*Ramschverkauf*
junk	*Müll*
keeper	*Aufpasser, Beschützer*
ladle	*Suppenkelle*
lager	*helles Bier*
land a job	*einen Job bekommen*
landlord	*Vermieter*
latter	*Letztere/r*
launch	*werfen, in Gang bringen*
law	*Gesetz*
lawyer	*Rechtsanwalt*
leaf through	*durchblättern*
leak out	*auslaufen, lecken*
left-back	*linker Vorstopper*
leftovers	*Reste, was übrig ist*
legally	*rechtmäßig, per Gesetz*
lift	*hochheben*
limit	*einschränken, limitieren; Begrenzung, Grenze, Limit*
lively	*lebendig*
loaf (of bread)	*Laib (Brot)*
local	*Kneipe*
log	*Holzscheit*
loop holes	*Schlupflöcher*
lot	*Mischpoke, Menschenschlag*
lousy	*jämmerlich, schlecht*
lumber	*schwerfällig bewegen*
mack (mackintosh)	*Regenmantel*
madness	*Wahnsinn*
maid	*Dienstmädchen*
majority	*Mehrheit*
make up	*herstellen, machen*
mark	*beachten, bedenken, hervorheben*

masterpiece	*Meisterwerk*
matter	*Angelegenheit*
mention	*Erwähnen*
meritocracy	*Leistungsgesellschaft*
message	*Nachricht*
messy	*durcheinander, dreckig*
metal detector	*Metalldetektor*
minor	*klein, geringfügig*
minority	*Minderheit*
misbehave	*schlecht benehmen, sich danebenbenehmen*
mistletoe	*Mistel*
mitigation	*Entlastung*
moan	*nölen, meckern*
mobile phone	*Handy*
moist	*feucht, nass*
monitor	*überwachen*
monkey	*Affe*
mood	*Laune*
mortgage	*Hypothek*
mud	*Matsch*
muddle through	*sich durchmauscheln*
mug	*überfallen*
multiplicity	*große Anzahl von, Vielzahl*
mundane	*mondän*
murder	*Mord*
mushroom	*(essbarer) Pilz*
negotiation	*Verhandlung*
night-cap	*Schlummertrunk*
nod	*nicken*
nose one's way	*sich seinen Weg bahnen*
notorious	*berüchtigt*
nourish	*ernähren*
numerous	*viele, unzählige*
oaken	*aus Eiche*
oblige	*verpflichten*

observation	*Beobachtung*
observe	*beobachten*
obvious	*offensichtlich*
occasionally	*gelegentlich*
oh crikey	*oh Mann*
on average	*durchschnittlich*
one for the road	*einen für unterwegs*
open-minded	*offen, liberal*
operating table	*OP-Tisch*
operating theatre	*Operationssaal, OP*
opposite	*Gegenteil*
ordinance survey	*detaillierte topografische Landkarten (wie beim Militär)*
originally	*ursprünglich, eigentlich*
overall	*Overall*
overdue	*überfällig*
overfed	*überfüttert*
overgrown	*überwachsen*
overshadow	*überschatten*
overweight	*Übergewicht*
overwhelmed	*überwältigt*
overworked	*überarbeitet*
pad (slang)	*Zuhause, Wohnung*
pale	*blass*
pamper	*verwöhnen*
panel	*Verkleidung, Verstrebung*
pastime	*Zeitvertreib*
patronise	*regelmäßig besuchen, hingehen*
per capita	*pro Kopf*
performance	*Leistung*
petal	*Blütenblatt*
petty theft	*leichter Diebstahl*
pick up	*abholen*
pile	*Stapel, große Menge*
pine	*Kiefer*
pint (of beer)	*Pint – etwa ein halber Liter*

pissed as a newt	*besoffen (voll wie eine Strandhaubitze)*
plot	*Verschwörung*
pluck	*zupfen, zerren*
plumber	*Klempner*
poison	*vergiften*
polite	*höflich*
pollution	*Verschmutzung*
portray	*darstellen, porträtieren*
pour	*gießen, kippen*
power failure	*Stromausfall*
predecessor	*Vorgänger*
premises	*Firmengelände*
prescription	*Rezept (vom Arzt)*
presume	*vermuten, annehmen*
pretend	*so tun, als ob*
price range	*Preisspanne*
print	*drucken*
prison record	*Gefängnisaufenthalte*
proclaim	*proklamieren, verkünden*
procrastinate	*zögern, zaudern*
prod	*anstacheln, ins Gedächtnis rufen*
profit	*Profit, Leistungsspanne*
profit from	*profitieren von*
progress	*Fortschritte machen*
promote	*vorantreiben, unterstützen*
promotion	*Beförderung*
protected bird	*(natur)geschützter Vogel*
proud	*stolz*
prove	*beweisen*
provoke	*provozieren*
pushy	*aufdringlich, penetrant*
quarrel	*Auseinandersetzung*
query	*(nach)fragen, sich erkundigen*
rarely	*selten*
receiver	*Hörer*

refer to	*beziehen auf, Bezug nehmen auf*
referral	*Überweisung*
refuge	*Rückzug*
refusal	*Weigerung*
reign	*regieren*
relationship	*Beziehung, Freundschaft*
reliable	*zuverlässig*
relief	*Erleichterung*
rent	*Miete*
rental contract	*Mietvertrag*
replace	*ersetzen*
represent	*darstellen, repräsentieren*
representative	*Repräsentant*
research	*Forschung*
reserved	*reserviert*
resist	*widerstehen*
resolution	*Vorsatz*
resolve	*entschließen*
responsible for	*verantwortlich für*
rest assured	*versichert sein*
resurrection	*(Wieder-)Auferstehung*
review	*(über)prüfen*
rob	*stehlen*
roughness	*Härte, Wildheit*
rub shoulders with	*Bekanntschaft machen mit*
rubber boot	*Gummistiefel*
rude	*ungehobelt, unhöflich*
sauce	*Sauce*
scale	*Ebene*
scenery	*Landschaft*
scent	*Geruch, Duft*
score	*Punkte machen*
scrap-merchant	*Schrotthändler*
scratch	*kratzen*
screech	*kreischen*
security guard	*Sicherheitsbeamter*

selfish	*selbstsüchtig, egoistisch*
self-mockery	*Selbstverspottung*
semi-detached house	*Doppelhaushälfte*
sensible	*vernünftig*
sensitive	*empfindlich*
sentence	*verurteilen*
separate the wheat from the chaff	*Spreu vom Weizen trennen*
series	*Reihe*
service	*instand halten*
set up	*errichten*
settle down	*sich niederlassen*
severe	*ernst*
shabby	*schäbig*
shadow	*Schatten*
shake	*schütteln*
shatter	*kaputtmachen, zerschlagen*
shed a tear	*eine Träne vergießen*
shell	*Schale*
shelves	*Regale*
short of money	*knapp bei Kasse*
sigh	*seufzen, stöhnen*
signal	*signalisieren, Zeichen geben*
signature	*Unterschrift*
silt	*Sand, Schlamm*
similarity	*Ähnlichkeit*
sliced	*in Scheiben geschnitten*
slim	*schlank*
slippery	*rutschig, glitschig*
slots	*Werbeeinspielungen*
smash	*zerstören, zerschlagen*
smell	*Geruch*
smut	*(unanständige) Zote*
snack	*Imbiss*
sniff	*schnüffeln*
snore	*schnarchen*
social benefits	*Sozialleistungen*

social conscience	*soziales Bewusstsein*
socialize	*unter Leute gehen, weggehen*
soil	*Boden, Erde*
somersault	*Purzelbaum*
sordid	*schmutzig, schäbig*
soul	*Seele*
spare	*ersparen, erübrigen*
spit	*spucken*
split	*spalten*
spoil	*verderben*
spoilt for choice	*Qual der Wahl*
spoon	*Löffel*
spouse	*Ehepartner*
spree	*Ausflug, Tour*
spy	*spionieren*
squelch	*platschen, glucksen*
stab	*stechen*
stagger	*stolpern, schwanken*
standing order	*Dauerauftrag*
stand-offish	*ablehnend, unnahbar*
starvation	*Hungern, Verhungern*
stationary	*stehen, sich nicht bewegen*
stepping stone	*Trittstein, Sprungbrett*
stocking	*Strumpf, der an den Kamin gehängt wird und in den vom Weihnachtsmann die Geschenke getan werden sollen*
stone	*Gewichtseinheit, etwa 6,3 kg*
stressful	*stressig, anstrengend*
strictness	*Härte, Rigidität*
stroke of luck	*Glückstreffer*
struggle	*kämpfen*
stuck on	*aufgesetzt, aufgespießt*
stuff	*stopfen, füllen*
subsidiary	*Tochtergesellschaft*
suburb	*Vorstadt, außerhalb gelegener Stadtteil*

suffer	*leiden*
supply	*Versorgung*
surface	*Oberfläche*
surgery hours	*Sprechstunde*
surly	*verdrießlich, mürrisch*
suspicious	*argwöhnisch*
sweep	*fegen*
sweetheart	*Liebling, Schatz*
swill	*gurgeln, schlucken*
swindle	*schwindeln, betrügen*
sympathetic	*mitfühlend*
tailor	*Schneider*
take the bull by the horns	*den Stier bei den Hörnern packen*
take turn for the better	*sich zum Besseren wenden*
takeaway	*zum Mitnehmen*
talk about the birds and the bees	*(Slang:) über Sex sprechen*
talk shop	*über das Geschäft reden*
talkative	*redselig*
tangle	*verwickeln, durcheinander geraten*
target	*Ziel*
tax adviser	*Steuerberater*
tax return	*Steuerklärung*
tear	*zerreißen, kaputtmachen; Träne*
temper	*Laune*
terms	*Konzepte, Ideen, Bedingungen*
terrace, terraced house	*Reihenhaus*
terrain	*Boden*
thread	*Faden*
throb	*pulsieren*
tie	*Schlips*
tiny	*winzig, klein*
tips	*Hinweise, Tipps*
to the utmost	*aufs äußerste, bis zum Geht-nichtmehr*
toot one's horn	*hupen*
towel	*Handtuch*

town-crier	*Ausrufer*
traffic	*Verkehr*
treatment	*Behandlung*
trial	*Gerichtsverhandlung*
trip up	*ein Bein stellen, stolpern*
tread on	*treten auf*
trolley	*(Einkaufs-)Wagen*
truck	*LKW*
truncheon	*Schlagstock, Knüppel*
trust	*vertrauen*
tune into	*einschalten (Radio)*
turn	*Reihe, dran sein*
turn up	*auftauchen*
twist	*ausrenken, verstauchen*
tyre	*Reifen*
unbearable	*untragbar*
uncomfortable	*unbequem, unangenehm*
unconscious	*bewusstlos*
underlying	*darunter liegend*
understaffed	*unterbesetzt*
undertaker	*Bestattungsunternehmer*
unearthly	*unchristlich, nachtschlafend*
unexpected	*unerwartet*
uninhabited	*unbewohnt*
untouched	*nicht angerührt, unberührt*
uproar	*Aufruhr*
upset	*aufgewühlt, verärgert*
utensils	*Utensilien, Ausrüstung*
vacation	*Urlaub*
variety	*Vielzahl*
vehicle	*Fahrzeug*
venison	*Wild (Fleisch)*
vicinity	*Umgebung*
violence	*Gewalt*
violent	*gewalttätig*
virtue	*Tugend*

waist	*Taille*
wallet	*Brieftasche*
wander	*schlendern, laufen*
warrant	*Fahndung, Suchbefehl*
waste	*Abfall*
waste water	*Abwasser*
wave	*winken, Welle*
wealth	*große Menge, Wohlstand*
wealthy	*wohlhabend*
weapon	*Waffe*
weigh	*wiegen*
well-dressed	*gut gekleidet*
well-heeled	*betucht, wohlhabend*
whisper	*flüstern*
whistle	*pfeifen, säuseln*
windy	*kurvenreich*
withdraw	*zurückziehen, zurücknehmen*
witness	*Zeuge*
worry	*sich sorgen*
would-be	*Möchtegern*
wounded	*verwundet*
you can't make a silk purse out of a sow's ear	*aus einem Kieselstein kann man keinen Diamanten schleifen*
your Honour	*Euer Ehren*